OBJECT-ORIENTED PROGRAMMING
WITH VISUAL BASIC.NET

Michael McMillan provides a complete presentation of the object-oriented features of the Visual Basic.NET language for advanced Visual Basic programmers. Beginning with an introduction to abstract data types and their initial implementation using structures, he explains standard object-oriented programming (OOP) topics including class design, inheritance, access modifiers and scoping issues, abstract classes, design and implementation of interfaces and design patterns, and refactoring in Visual Basic.NET. More advanced OOP topics are included as well, such as reflection, object persistence, and serialization.

To tie everything together, McMillan demonstrates sound OOP design and implementation principles through practical examples of standard Windows applications, database applications using ADO.NET, Web-based applications using ASP.NET, and Windows service applications.

Michael McMillan is Instructor of Computer Information Systems at Pulaski Technical College. With more than twenty years of experience in the computer industry, he has written numerous articles for trade journals such as *Software Development* and *Windows NT Systems*. He is author of *Perl from the Ground Up* and coauthor of several books including *Programming and Problem Solving with Visual Basic.NET* and *A Laboratory Course in Visual Basic.NET*.

OBJECT-ORIENTED
PROGRAMMING WITH
VISUAL BASIC.NET

MICHAEL McMILLAN
Pulaski Technical College, North Little Rock, Arkansas

CAMBRIDGE
UNIVERSITY PRESS

PUBLISHED BY THE PRESS SYNDICATE OF THE UNIVERSITY OF CAMBRIDGE
The Pitt Building, Trumpington Street, Cambridge, United Kingdom

CAMBRIDGE UNIVERSITY PRESS
The Edinburgh Building, Cambridge CB2 2RU, UK
40 West 20th Street, New York, NY 10011-4211, USA
477 Williamstown Road, Port Melbourne, VIC 3207, Australia
Ruiz de Alarcón 13, 28014 Madrid, Spain
Dock House, The Waterfront, Cape Town 8001, South Africa

http://www.cambridge.org

First published 2004

Printed in the United States of America

Typefaces ITC Berkeley Oldstyle 11/13.5 pt. and ITC Franklin Gothic   *System* LaTeX 2_ε [TB]

A catalog record for this book is available from the British Library.

Library of Congress Cataloging in Publication Data
McMillan, Michael, 1957–
    Object-oriented programming with Visual Basic.Net / Michael McMillan
        p.   cm.
    Includes bibliographical references and index.
    ISBN 0-521-53983-8 (pb.)
    1. Object-oriented programming (Computer science)   2. Microsoft Visual BASIC.
    3. BASIC (Computer program language)   4. Microsoft.NET.   I. Title
    QA76.64.M389   2004
    005.1'17 – dc22   2003055949

ISBN 0 521 53983 8 paperback

Contents

Preface

Visual Basic is arguably the most popular application development programming language in use today. Thousands, if not millions, of programmers use it every day to build both commercial and scientific applications. The language is also one of the most maligned programming languages, second perhaps only to Cobol.

The newest version of Visual Basic, Visual Basic.NET (VB.NET), should eventually quiet many of those who call Visual Basic a toy language. Microsoft performed a major redesign of Visual Basic and added many features that put the language on equal footing with the other major .NET language, C#, and with other contemporary languages, especially Java.

One area of the language that has seen significant improvement is VB.NET's object-oriented programming features. In previous versions of Visual Basic, many of these features were partially implemented, not implemented at all, or implemented in a wrong-headed manner. VB.NET provides the programmer with a complete set of object-oriented tools. This book explains in detail how to use these features.

The book is informally partitioned into three parts. Chapters 1 through 6 present the fundamentals of object-oriented programming (OOP) using VB.NET. Chapter 1 provides a review of the syntax of VB.NET. This chapter is especially useful for readers who have experience with an older version of Visual Basic. Chapter 2 discusses the philosophy of OOP, including some sections on object-oriented design and abstract data types. Chapter 3 covers programming with structures, which are similar to user-defined types (UDTs) in Visual Basic 6. Structures are more powerful than UDTs because you can also define subprograms (methods) within a structure definition.

Chapter 4 introduces the reader to classes and covers all the fundamental components of a class—data members, constructors, property methods, and other methods. Chapter 5 discusses the different access modifiers (Public, Private, Protected, and Friend) that can be applied to class objects, data members, and methods. Understanding how access modifiers work is important for creating a properly functioning object-oriented program. Chapter 6 ends the first part of the book by examining how to create abstract classes and interfaces in VB.NET. Inheritance is a very important concept in OOP, and one that is easy for the newcomer to misunderstand. By combining the two major types of inheritance in one chapter, the reader can more easily compare and contrast inheritance versus interfaces to decide which to use for any particular application.

Chapter 7 begins the coverage of more advanced OOP topics by examining two interfaces that are frequently implemented in a class: IEnumerable and IComparable. The IEnumerable interface is used when class objects are placed into a collection, and the IComparable interface is used to compare complex class objects that are made up of more than one primitive data type. Chapter 8 covers exception handling in VB.NET, including how to build custom exception classes to enable a class to throw its own exceptions rather than rely on built-in exceptions.

Chapter 9 discusses two software engineering aspects of OOP—design patterns and refactoring. These techniques are becoming more and more important to building OOP applications and no introduction to OOP would be complete without discussing how to use design patterns and refactoring in making programs more efficient and more maintainable. Chapter 10 examines how reflection can be used to examine a class at runtime and how to invoke a class method without using an instance of the class. Chapter 11 introduces the reader to how serialization is used for object persistence. Persistence is the ability of a class to save its state from one invocation of an object to another.

The third section of the book consists of Chapters 12 and 13, which demonstrate how to use OOP techniques to build Windows applications. Chapter 12 discusses using OOP on a standard, form-based application and Chapter 13 examines how to use OOP and ADO.NET for designing programs that interact with a database.

This book is intended as a second course, or text, in the VB.NET language. The reader should at least be familiar with the basic constructs (sequence, branching, loops, subprograms, and event handling) of the programming languages that are currently popular (i.e., Visual Basic, C++, or Java). One of the strengths of this book is that it does not try to combine teaching the fundamentals of the VB.NET language along with the language's OOP features. Although some OOP purists might disagree, I believe that the programming student should fully understand the imperative paradigm before attempting to learn the object-oriented paradigm.

The book can be used as a textbook in a second or third course in VB.NET or in conjunction with another, more traditional textbook, and it can be read for self-study. Each chapter has a set of exercises that all readers should attempt to complete. If you are an instructor and would like solutions to the exercises, please email me at mmcmillan@pulaskitech.edu and we will begin a correspondence so that I can determine whether you are indeed an instructor and not an enterprising student.

CHAPTER 1

An Overview of the Visual Basic.NET Language

This chapter presents an overview of the syntax and primary constructs of the Visual Basic.NET (VB.NET) language for programmers unfamiliar with VB.NET. This is not a tutorial chapter, however, so if you are new to programming you should study another text on VB.NET before continuing with this book. If, though, you are coming to VB.NET from some other language, such as C++ or Java or even Visual Basic 6, you should read through this chapter to familiarize yourself with the language.

NET PROGRAMS

There are two ways to build programs in VB.NET. One is to use the Visual Studio.NET Integrated Development Environment (IDE). The other is to use the command-line compiler packaged as part of the .NET Framework Software Development Kit (SDK). In this section we'll discuss developing programs with the command-line compiler, since this software is free and can run on any of the modern Windows operating sysems (Windows 98 and beyond).

VB.NET Program Types

With VB.NET, you can write many different kinds of programs. A VB.NET program that makes use of a graphical user interface (GUI) is a Windows application. A VB.NET program that uses the command-prompt console for input and output is called a Console application. You can also write Internet applications, Windows Services applications, and other types of applications. In this book we will focus on Console and Windows applications, though we will look at examples of Windows Services and Internet (ASP.NET) applications in the last few chapters.

Writing a Console Application Using the Command-Line Compiler

You do not have to be running Visual Studio.NET to compile and run VB.NET programs. A command-line compiler is shipped with the .NET Framework and can be used for any VB.NET programs you want to develop.

To get to the compiler, find the Microsoft.NET subdirectory. It is usually found in the Winnt or Windows (for Windows 98) directory. Then change directories to the Framework subdirectory. The compiler resides in yet another subdirectory. The name of the subdirectory depends on which version of the .NET Framework you are using. The current .NET Framework version stores the compiler in the v1.0.3705 subdirectory, but be sure to check this on your own system since your version may be different. The path to the compiler for a typical computer running Windows 2000 is c:\winnt\Microsoft.NET\Framework\v1.0.3705.

Using the compiler is quite simple. First, create a source file using the text editor of your choice. Make sure the file you create has a .vb extension. Let's look at an example of a simple VB.NET program, a program that displays the text "Hello, world!" on the screen:

```
Imports System
Module HelloWorld
  Sub Main()
    Console.WriteLine("Hello, world!")
  End Sub
End Module
```

The first line indicates that the program needs to use a class found in the System *namespace*. A namespace is a tool used to group related classes and other types together. Namespaces also allow different classes to share the same name. Using the keyword Imports allows us to use a class from the specified namespace (System in this case) without using the namespace name first. We can just as easily leave the first line of the program out altogether and type in the fully qualified name of the class:

```
System.Console.WriteLine("Hello, world!")
```

Generally, importing a namespace makes your programs easier to write and easier to read.

The next line defines a module named HelloWorld. A *module* is one of the possible packages into which we can write code that we want to compile and execute. Another package we can use is a class. Generally, though, we want to save the use of classes for defining our own custom types, so we'll use modules for writing Console applications in this book. Modules are begun with the Module keyword and are closed with the line End Sub.

The first line inside the Module definition defines a subroutine called Main. This subroutine is the entry point of the application, and the compiler will report an error if Main is not found somewhere in a module or class. If you are using a class rather than a module as the packaging for your application, Main must be defined as a Shared method, which means that the class does not have to be instantiated for the code to be executed. We'll explain later in the book what we mean by a Shared method. Main must be closed with the line End Sub.

The line that displays the message "Hello, world!" on the display is

```
Console.WriteLine("Hello, world!")
```

To display text on the computer's console, you have to call the Console class and the proper method for writing text to the console, one of which is the WriteLine method. This method displays the text passed to it as the argument on the console and then writes a newline character so that any more text will be written on the next line.

To end this section, we'll look at writing the same HelloWorld program as a class rather than as a module. The codes are similar, and to be honest, the two techniques are virtually identical. However, because in this book we use classes to define special types, we'll write all our Console applications as modules.

Here's the HelloWorld class code:

```
Imports System
Class HelloWorld
  Shared Sub Main()
    Console.WriteLine("Hello, world!")
  End Sub
End class
```

To compile your program (assuming the source file name is test.vb), issue the following command:

```
vbc test.vb
```

If your program compiles successfully, you can simply run the executable file (test.exe) to run it. If your program has errors in it, the compiler will return the errors to your console.

Writing a Windows Application Using the Command-Line Compiler

One of the surprising things about VB.NET is that you don't have to use Visual Studio.NET to build a Windows application. Unlike previous versions of the language, VB.NET gives the programmer the ability to build a GUI directly from code. Although you probably won't want to use this feature all that often, there will be situations when building a GUI from scratch will be necessary. This is certainly true if you are using Windows 98 or ME and can't run Visual Studio.NET.

To demonstrate how to write a Windows application, we'll rewrite the HelloWorld program so that the text is displayed in a label on a form. First, let's look at the code:

```
Imports System
Imports System.Drawing
Imports System.Windows.Forms

Public Class HelloWorld
  Inherits Form
```

```
Private lblHelloLabel As Label

Public Shared Sub Main()
  Application.Run(New HelloWorld())
End Sub

Public Sub New()
  lblHelloLabel = New Label()
  With lblHelloLabel
    .Location = New Point(50, 50)
    .Size = New Size(392, 64)
    .Font = New Font("Courier", 24)
    .Text = "Hello, world!"
    .TabIndex = 0
    .TextAlign = ContentAlignment.TopCenter
  End With

  Me.Text = "A Hello, world! Windows Example"
  AutoScaleBaseSize = New Size(10, 20)
  FormBorderStyle = FormBorderStyle.FixedSingle
  ClientSize = New Size(599, 125)

  Controls.Add(lblHelloLabel)

  End Sub
End Class
```

You'll notice first that there are two new namespaces imported into the program. These namespaces are needed for building Windows applications. The next line is just the definition of the class that holds the program. The following line

```
Inherits Form
```

tells the compiler that the HelloWorld class is inheriting the Form class, which is found in the Systems.Windows.Forms namespace. *Inheritance* is a powerful technique in object-oriented programming and we will spend at least one chapter discussing it later in the book.

The next line declares a label for displaying the "Hello, world!" text. Following this declaration is the Main subroutine. Be sure to use the Shared modifier in the heading since we have to use a class for a Windows application.

The single line inside Sub Main is

```
Application.Run(New HelloWorld())
```

The Application class (which is part of System.Windows.Forms) includes the Run method, which performs the tasks necessary to run the HelloWorld program as a Windows application.

Following Sub Main is another subroutine definition—New. The New subroutine is a special type called a *constructor*. Constructors are used to create a new Class object. This process is called *instantiation* and every new Class object must be instantiated using a constructor. The code inside the constructor definition is run when the constructor is called, which in this program is the line

```
Application.Run(New HelloWorld())
```

Constructors are discussed in much more detail in Chapter 4.

Inside the constructor method are the details for displaying "Hello, world!" in a form. First, a new label is instantiated. We'll place our text inside this label. The next several lines set several of the label's properties, including the font type, the font size, and the location of the label. These lines are placed inside a With statement, a convenient shortcut to use when you need to make several changes to or perform other operations on the same object.

The line after the End With statement sets the caption of the current form. Since there isn't really a name for the form, we refer to it as Me. We'll see other uses for Me throughout the book.

The next three lines set some properties having to do with our form. The last line before the end of the subroutine adds the label to the form's Control collection. The program ends by closing off the subroutine definition and the class definition.

Windows applications are compiled a little differently than Console applications. The command to compile the HelloWorld program is as follows:

```
vbc HelloWorld.vb /reference:System.dll,System.Drawing._
dll, System.Windows.Forms.dll /target:winexe
```

(Note that the command would be all one line when typed, but here it is broken into two lines for readability.)

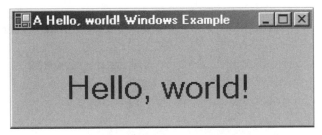

FIGURE 1.1. A Hello, World Windows Example

The first thing you notice is the switch—/reference. We have to add references to the different namespaces we use in this program for creating a Windows application. We didn't need this switch in the Console application because the compiler automatically includes the System.dll file. The other files (including System.dll), though, must be referenced specifically.

The last part of the command tells the compiler to build a Windows application (winexe). A Console application is compiled to just an .exe file. If you look at the file created by the compiler, though, it still displayed as wtest.exe. The compiler adds data internally to the file to enable it as a Windows application.

Now we're ready to run the program and examine the output (see Figure 1.1).

Data Types and Variables

VB.NET contains the standard data types for storing numeric, string, character, and object values, as well as special data types for times, dates, and monetary values. The primary data types in VB.NET are the following:

- **Boolean:** True or False.
- **Byte:** 0–255 (unsigned).
- **Char:** 0–65535 (unsigned).
- **Date:** A date and time combination.
- **Decimal:** 0 through $\pm$79,228,162,514,264,337,593,543,950,335 with no decimal point; 0 through $\pm$7.9228162514264337593543950335 with 28 places to the right of the decimal; smallest nonzero number is $\pm$0.0000000000000000000000000001 ($\pm$1E$-$28).

- **Double:** −1.79769313486231570E+308 through −4.94065645841246544E−324 for negative values; 4.94065645841246544E−324 through 1.79769313486231570E+308 for positive values.
- **Integer:** −2,147,483,648 through 2,147,483,647.
- **Long:** −9,223,372,036,854,775,808 through 9,223,372,036,854,775,807.
- **Object:** Any object.
- **Short:** −32,768 through 32,767.
- **Single:** −3.4028235E+38 through −1.401298E−45 for negative values; 1.401298E−45 through 3.4028235E+38 for positive values.
- **String:** 0 to approximately 2 billion Unicode characters.
- **Structure:** A user-defined type built from other data type components.

Variable Declaration

Variables are declared using the Dim keyword. For example,

```
Dim mySalary As Integer
Dim empID As String
```

The reason we use the Dim keyword when declaring a variable dates back to the early days of the Basic language. In those days, variables did not have to be declared; they could just pop into existence when needed. Arrays, however, had to declared first with the dimension of the array. The Dim keyword, then, identified a variable as an array and not just a plain variable. The use of Dim has continued through the many different versions of the language right up to VB.NET.

Multiple variables of the same type can be declared on the same line by separating each variable with a comma, like this:

```
Dim num1, num2, num3, num4 As Single
```

Initializers

An *initializer* is a variable declaration in which a value is also assigned to the variable. Initalizers are new to VB.NET, although many other languages have them. Here are some examples of initializers:

```
Dim salary As Integer = 35000
Dim lastName As String = "Durrwood"
```

Named Constants

A named constant is a variable whose value is assigned when it is declared and whose value cannot be changed. Named constants are often called "magic" values because they are usually used to represent important and/or frequently used values in a program.

Named constants are declared with the Const keyword. Here are some examples:

```
Const PI As Single = 3.14159
Const GREETING As String = "Hello, there."
Const LOGIN_CODE As String = :"letmein"
```

It is a common programming practice, though not a requirement of the VB.NET compiler, to use all uppercase letters when declaring a named constant. This helps these "magic" values stand out in your code so that they're easier to find.

Implicit Type Conversions and the Option Strict Switch

There are two ways to perform data type conversions in VB.NET. One way is to simply let the compiler do it for you. This is the easiest way and the one that is most likely to lead to both subtle and not-so-subtle errors in your programs. As an example, let's look at a simple code fragment that converts a Single value to an Integer:

```
Dim pi As Single = 3.14159
Dim intPi As Integer = pi
```

Because intPi is an Integer variable, when it is assigned the value of pi the compiler assigns the value 3 to the variable. This is called a *narrowing conversion* because the value 3.14159... is "narrowed" to 3 to fit in an Integer variable.

There are also *widening conversions*. When an Integer value is stored in a Single or Double variable, the value increases in size (widens) to hold the places to the right of the decimal point. Consider the following code fragment:

```
Dim intVal As Integer = 3
Dim dblVal As Double = intVal
```

Here an Integer variable storing the value 256 is assigned to a Double variable, so that the value 256.0 is stored in the Double. These types of conversions are called *implicit conversions* because the compiler performs the conversion behind the scenes.

Although implicit conversions are allowed, as just shown, that's not to say we should prefer allowing the compiler to make conversions for us. There will be situations when implicit conversions are made that are not what we want to happen, leading to logical errors or worse. The VB.NET compiler allows implicit conversions to take place when the Option Strict switch is off.

This switch tells the compiler whether or not to perform strict type checking. When Option Strict is off, implicit conversions will be performed; when Option Strict is on, a design-time error is flagged when an implicit conversion is attempted. Most, though certainly not all, programmers consider it good programming practice to set the Option Strict switch on so that any conversions that take place must be explicitly performed using a conversion function.

The Option Strict switch is set by writing either Option Strict On or Option Strict Off at the beginning of your program. In fact, the statement must precede any declarations or Imports statements, like this:

```
Option Strict On
Imports System
Module Module1
  Sub Main()
    ' Code here
  End Sub
End Module
```

One more word of caution on leaving the Option Strict switch off. It can lead to slower code. A simple example will illustrate the problem:

```
Dim n As Object
Dim names As String
For Each n In NameList
  names & = n & ","
Next
```

In this code, NameList is an ArrayList that holds a list of names. The loop builds a comma-delimited string of the names in the ArrayList. With Option Strict off, this code compiles and runs because the compiler will convert each value of n to a String before appending it to names. And that's the problem with leaving Option Strict off. Each conversion will take more time than necessary because the compiler has to perform a test of the data types and then perform the conversion. An explicit conversion via a conversion function will speed this up considerably. In the next section we'll examine how to perform explicit type conversions using VB.NET's type conversion functions.

Type Conversion Functions

VB.NET has a full set of built-in conversion functions for performing explicit type conversions. The following list shows each function and the type converted to:

- CBool: Boolean
- CByte: Byte
- CChar: Char
- CDate: Date
- CDbl: Double
- CDec: Decimal
- CInt: Integer
- CLng: Long
- CObj: Object
- CSng: Single
- CStr: String

Now let's look at some examples:

```
Salary = CInt(Console.ReadLine()) ' Converts console
                                  ' input to Integer
                                  ' value
```

```
Salary = CInt(txtSalary.Text) ' Does the same with a
                              ' textbox
taxRate = CDbl(5)
```

There are many other type conversions you can perform that are not as intuitive as these. For example, you can convert from a Boolean value to a String. The Boolean values True and False become "True" and "False" after the conversion. You can convert an Integer to Boolean—zero converts to False and a nonzero value converts to True.

Arrays

There are many times when you need to store related values within one variable name. Since regular variables only allow you to store one value in them at a time, you have to use something else—an *array*.

An array is a variable that stores multiple values of the same data type. Each value in an array (also called an element) is indexed by number. Arrays are created by specifying an array name, the number of elements to store, and the data type of the elements. The general form for an array declaration is

```
Dim array-name(n) As Data-type
```

Here are some array declaration examples:

```
Dim grades(9) As Integer
Dim names(39) As String
Dim averages(99) As Single
```

In VB.NET, as in of most other languages, the first index of an array is 0. For that reason, the number you use to declare the size of an array should always be one less than the total number of elements you want to store in the array. In the preceding examples, the grades array stores 10 elements, the names array stores 40 elements, and the averages array stores 100 elements.

An alternative way to declare an array is to provide an initialization list, which is a list of values to store in the array. The values are separated by commas and surrounded within curly braces. Here is an example:

```
Dim grades() As Integer = {65, 72, 83, 97}
```

The compiler automatically sizes the array based on the number of items in the initialization list. Putting a number inside the parentheses after the array name will lead to an exception.

Array objects are treated like class instances in VB.NET. There is a set of methods associated with arrays you can use in your programming. One of the most useful of these methods is GetUpperBound. This method returns the last index number (referencing the last element) in an array. You can use this method when looping through an array, which is demonstrated later in this chapter when we discuss repetition statements.

There are also array methods that perform tasks that used to take specially written code to perform, such as sorting an array and reversing an array. The two methods for these operations are Sort and Reverse. Here's an example:

```
Imports System
Module Array
  Sub Main()
    Dim names() As String = {"Mike", "Francis", "Ed", _
                             "Joan", "Terri"}
    names.Sort(names)
    Dim name As String
    For Each name In names
      Console.Write(name & " ")
    Next
    names.Reverse(names)
    Console.WriteLine()
    For Each name In names
      Console.Write(name & " ")
    Next
  End Sub
End Module
```

Multi-dimensional Arrays

Arrays are not limited to one dimension. You can create arrays of multiple dimensions, though it is uncommon to see arrays of more than three dimensions. The most common multidimensional arrays are two-dimensional arrays that model a table of data.

A two-dimensional array creates a set of data in the form of rows and columns. The rows make up the first, or 0th, dimension of the array, and the columns make up the second, or 1st, dimension of the array. The general form of a two-dimensional array declaration is

```
Dim array-name(rows, cols) As Data-type
```

For example, the following code declares an Integer array with five rows and six columns:

```
Dim nums(4,5) As Integer
```

You can also use an initialization list in a two-dimensional array declaration. Each dimension is delimited by curly braces and separated from each other by a column. Here's an example:

```
Dim grades(,) As Integer = {{76, 83, 91}, {100, 75, 66}}
```

Within the parentheses is a single comma. This comma indicates to the compiler that the array should be created with two dimensions. An array created with three dimensions would have two commas.

Array Element Access

Array elements are accessed by referencing their position in the array by index number. For example, the 0th element of a single-dimensional array named grades is accessed like this:

```
current_grade = grades(0)
```

Accessing an element in a two-dimensional array is similar:

```
current_grade = grades(1, 3)   ' Accesses grade in second
                               ' row, fourth column
```

You can assign data to an array element in the same way:

```
grades(0) = 82
grades(1,3) = 94
```

Processing Array Elements

The most interesting processing you can do with arrays involves looping constructs, which we haven't discussed yet. We will look at examples of processing arrays when we cover loops later in this chapter.

ARITHMETIC, STRING, AND RELATIONAL OPERATORS

VB.NET provides a full set of operators for performing arithmetic, operations on strings, and other processes. In this section we'll review these operators.

Arithmetic Operators

The arithmetic operators are the following:

*   + (addition)
*   - (subtraction)
*   * (multiplication)
*   / (division)
*   \ (integer division)
*   Mod (modulo)

The first four operators should be familiar to you. We will not discuss them here. The last two operators, however, might be new to those who don't have much of a mathematics background.

When one operand is divided by a second operand using the integer division operator, the result is rounded up to the integer nearest zero. The modulo operator, in contrast, returns the remainder of the division of two operands. Next we look at some examples using these operators.

```
result = 4 \ 2.25  ' result is assigned the value 2
result = 23 mod 2  ' result is assigned the value 1
```

String Operators

There are two string operators in VB.NET and they both perform the same operation—concatenation. These operators are the ampersand (&) and the plus sign (+). Generally, you should choose the ampersand when performing string concatenation in order to make your intentions obvious, but be aware that using the plus sign will work also. Here are some examples:

```
Dim new_string As String
Dim string1, string2, string3 As String
string1 = "Object-Oriented Programming "
string2 = "With Visual Basic.NET"
new_string = string1 & string2
new_string = new_string & " Edition " + "1"
Console.WriteLine(new_string)
```

The value of new_string is "Object-Oriented Programming With Visual Basic.NET Edition 1". If you remove the quotes from "1", an error results because the + sign is defined only for concatenation when a string is one of the operands.

Special Relational Operators and Logical Operators

VB.NET features the normal complement of relational operators necessary for modifying the control flow of a program and for performing comparisons between two operands. These are discussed below when we discuss branching statements.

There are also some special relational operators used with referency types in VB.NET. These special relational operators are:

- Is (For testing reference types for equality)
- TypeOf . . . Is (For testing to see if a reference type is a particular type)
- Like (For string comparisons using pattern matching)

The Is operator is used to test the equality of reference objects. Quite often, the Is operator is used to determine if a reference object has been "de-referenced" or set to Nothing. The TypeOf . . . Is operator is used to determine if a reference object is a specific type. The program below demonstrates how these operators are used:

```
Module Module1

  Public Class Name
    Private first As String
    Private last As String

    Public Sub New()
      first = ""
      last = ""
    End Sub
  End Class
  Sub Main()
    Dim myName As New Name()
    If (TypeOf (myName) Is Name) Then
      Console.WriteLine("Object is a Name type")
    End If
    myName = Nothing
    If (myName Is Nothing) Then
      Console.WriteLine("Object is now nothing.")
    End If
    Console.Read()
  End Sub

End Module
```

The Like operator performs pattern matching on strings in order to perform "close matches." For example, if you need to determine if a string begins with a certain two characters, but can contain any other characters after those two, you can write a statement like this:

```
If (name Like "Mi*") Then...
```

The rules for determining matches using the Like operator are as follows:

- The ? character matches any single character.
- The * character matches zero or more characters.
- The # character matches any single digit.

- The [ ] brackets indicate that any characters withing the brackets match any single character.

Branching Statements

There are two statements used for branching in VB.NET: the If statement and the Select Case statement. In this section, we'll look at the various ways you can form an If statement and then look at how to perform more structured branching using the Select Case statement.

The If Statement

Branching is the term used for altering the flow of a computer program based on testing a value or set of values. For example, when writing a program that calculates a company's payroll, the program should perform one set of calculations if an employee has worked forty hours or less and the program should perform a different set of calculations if an employee has worked more than forty hours. Branching is most commonly performed in VB.NET with the *If* statement.

The most common form of an If statement is:

```
If (expression) Then
   Statement body
End If
```

The expression inside parentheses is always an expression that evaluates to True or False. The expression is usually formed using one or more of the following relational operators:

- > (greater than)
- >= (greater than or equal to)
- < (less than)
- <= (less than or equal to)
- = (equal to)
- <> (not equal to)

Expressions using these operators are often called *relational expressions*. Examples of these types of expressions would be:

```
(hours > 40)
(salary = 35000)
(myName <> yourName)
```

Relational expressions can be combined using one of the *logical operators*. These operators are used to combine two or more relational expressions that evaluate to one truth value. The logical operators are:

- And
- Or
- Not

Here are some examples of relational expressions combined with logical operators:

```
(hours > 40) Or (salary > 22000)
(pwd = "Guess") And (id = "Admin")
Not (time = 1300)
```

When the expression tested by an If statement is True, the statement(s) inside the body of the If are executed. If the expression is False, the statement body is skipped and control passes to the line after the end of the If statement. Here's an example:

```
hours = 42
If (hours > 40) Then
   pay = (hours * (salary * 1.5))
End If
```

Often, when writing an If statement, you want to perform one set of operations if the expression is True and another set of operations if the expression is False. To do this, use the If–Else form of the If statement:

```
If (expression) Then
   Statement body
Else
   Statement body
End If
```

We can use this form of the If statement in the previous example to calculate an employee's pay based on how many hours he or she worked:

```
If (hours > 40) Then
  pay = hours * (salary * 1.5)
Else
  pay = hours * salary
End If
```

If statements can be nested inside other If statements if necessary, though this often leads to logic that is hard to understand. Here's an example extending the payroll code we've been looking at:

```
If (hours > 40) Then
  If (hours >= 50) Then
    pay = hours * (salary * 2.0)
  Else
    pay = hours * (salary * 1.5)
  End If
Else
  pay = hours * salary
End If
```

If an employee's hours are greater than 40 and the hours are greater than or equal to 50, then the employee is paid double time. If the hours are just greater than 40, then the employee is just paid time and a half. If neither of these are true, then the employee is just paid for regular time.

There is one final form of the If statement you can use when there are many possible choices to test. This form is the If–ElseIf:

```
If (expression) Then
  Statement body
ElseIf (expression) Then
  Statement body
ElseIf (expression) Then
  Statement body
Else
  Statement body
End If
```

Each expression is tested in order. If the first expression is True, then the statement body for that expression is executed and control passes to the statement after the End If statement. If the first expression is False, then the second expression is tested. If it is True, then the statement body is executed and control passes out of the If statement. This continues until there are no more expressions to test. If no expressions are True and there is an Else clause, the statement body within the Else is executed. Otherwise, the If statement is finished executing and the program continues.

Here's some code using the If–ElseIf form:

```
If (hours < 20) Then
   pay = hours * salary
ElseIf (hours > 20) And (hours <= 40) Then
   pay = (hours * salary)
   pay = pay - deductions
ElseIf (hours > 40) Then
   pay = hours * (salary * 1.5)
   pay = pay - deductions
End If
```

Short-Circuiting

When you combine two logical expressions with a logical operator, the compiler follows the standard "truth table" rules for determining whether the entire expression is True or False. For example, the expression

```
(12 > 23) Or (33 < 100)
```

is True because the first expression is True, making the whole expression True.

Since only the first expression need be tested in an Or expression, it makes sense to design the logical operators so that they'll recognize this situation and return True as soon as the compiler recognizes the operator to be Or and that the first expression is True. This is called short-circuiting, and VB.NET has two special logical operators for short-circuiting: AndAlso and OrElse.

Let's look first at OrElse. Here, if the first expression evaluates to True, the compiler can assign True to the complete expression and move on, as in the following example:

```
Dim grade1 As Integer = 92
Dim grade2 As Integer = 100
```

```
If (grade1 > 90 OrElse grade2 > 90) Then
  Console.WriteLine("Exempt from final.")
End If
```

The compiler doesn't have to test the expression grade2 > 90 since grade1 > 90 is True. If the value of grade1 is less than 90, making the first expression False, then the compiler must continue on to test the second expression.

The AndAlso operator works similarly, but with different rules, of course. Here's a code fragment that demonstrates how AndAlso works:

```
Dim FirstName As String = ""
Dim LastName As String = "Lennon"
If (FirstName <> "" AndAlso LastName <> "") Then
  Console.WriteLine("Name section complete.")
Else
  Console.WriteLine("Name section incomplete. Please _
                    finish.")
End If
```

The output from this code is

```
Name section incomplete. Please finish.
```

because the first expression in the If statement is False. The second expression is not even tested since both expressions must be True for the whole expression to be True.

The Select Case Statement

When you have a long series of expressions to test, a more structured way to write the code is to use a *Select Case* statement. The general form of the Select Case statement is

```
Select Case value
  Case (expression 1)
    Statement body
  Case (expression 2)
    Statement body
  Case (expression n)
    Statement body
```

```
   Case Else
      Statement body
End Select
```

The *value* at the beginning of the statement can be any expression that evaluates to a value. Each Case clause then tests an expression against the value, evaluating to either True or False. If True, the statement body inside the Case clause is executed and control is passed to the first statement after the Select Case statement; if False, the next Case clause is evaluated. If none of the expressions evaluate to True, and there is a Case Else clause, the statement body inside the clause is executed. If there is not a Case Else clause, and none of the expressions evaluate to True, control transfers to the first statement outside the Select Case statement.

Let's look at an example of using a Select Case statement. The following code fragment assumes a value has been assigned to the variable grade:

```
Select Case grade
   Case 90 To 100
      Console.WriteLine("You made an A!")
   Case 80 To 89
      Console.WriteLine("You made a B!")
   Case 70 To 79
      Console.WriteLine("You made a C.")
   Case 60 To 69
      Console.WriteLine("You made a D.")
   Case Is < 60
      Console.WriteLine("Sorry. You failed.")
   Case Else
      Console.WriteLine("Bad input.")
End Select
```

There are many different ways to test the value in the Select Case statement. One way, as just shown, is to use the To keyword to express a range of values that the tested value can fall within. You can also write out individual values, separating them with commas, like this:

```
Case 96, 97, 98, 99, 100
   Console.WriteLine("You made an A+!")
Case 90 To 95
```

```
Console.WriteLine("You made an A!")
. . .
```

You can use a relational operator in the Case clause, as we did in the earlier example to test for a failing grade. Here is another example, where all we're looking for is a passing or a failing grade:

```
Imports System
Module SelectCase
   Sub Main()
     Dim grade As Integer
     Console.Write("Enter your grade: ")
     grade = CInt(Console.ReadLine)
     Select Case grade
       Case Is >= 60
         Console.WriteLine("You passed!")
       Case Is < 60
         Console.WriteLine("Sorry, you failed.")
       Case Else
         Console.WriteLine("Bad input.")
     End Select
   End Sub
End Module
```

The Select Case statement should be used whenever you would have to write a very long If–ElseIf statement or whenever you want your branching code to be as readable as possible.

Repetition Statements

Another way the flow of control of a computer program can be altered is with repetition. Repetition allows a set of statements to be executed several times in succession, in essence executing the statements in a loop. There are several different types of looping statements in VB.NET. We will divide them into two categories—*While* loops and *For* loops.

The While Statement
The While statement loops through a set of statements "while" a tested expression is True. The loop only stops when the expression becomes False. The

general form of a While statement is

```
While (expression)
   Statement body
End While
```

Let's look at an example. If we want to determine how fast a city's population will grow over a period of years at a certain growth rate, we can do so with a While statement. Here's the code:

```
Imports System
Module Loops
   Sub Main()
      Dim growth As Single = 1.03
      Dim population As Single = 150000
      Dim numYears, start As Integer
      start = 1
      Console.Write("Enter the years of growth: ")
      numYears = CInt(Console.ReadLine)
      Console.WriteLine("The current population is: " & _
                  population)
      While (start <= numYears)
        population *= growth
        start += 1
      End While
      Console.WriteLine("The population will be: " & _
                  population & " after " & _
                  numYears & " years.")
   End Sub
End Module
```

The Do While Statement
An alternative way to write a While statement is to use the Do While statement. These two looping statements are functionally equivalent and can be used interchangeably. The general form of the Do While statement is

```
Do While (expression)
   Statement body
Loop
```

Here's the city growth example rewritten with a Do While statement:

```
Imports System
Module Loops
  Sub Main()
    Dim growth As Single = 1.03
    Dim population As Single = 150000
    Dim numYears, start As Integer
    start = 1
    Console.Write("Enter the years of growth: ")
    numYears = CInt(Console.ReadLine)
    Console.WriteLine("The current population is: " & _
                  population)
    Do While (start <= numYears)
      population *= growth
      start += 1
    Loop
    Console.WriteLine("The population will be: " & _
                  population & " after " & _
                  numYears & " years.")
  End Sub
End Module
```

The Do. . .Loop While Statement

There are often times when you want your loop test expression to be at the bottom of a loop. The *Do. . .Loop While* statement puts the test expression at the bottom of the statement, as shown here in its general form:

```
Do
  Statement body
Loop While (expression)
```

An example of an opportune time to use a Do. . .Loop While statement is when you are testing user input. The following code fragment prompts a user to enter his or her password and then tests this entry against the system password, looping back to have the user enter the password again if the tested password is incorrect:

```
Console.Write("Enter your password: ")
password = Console.ReadLine
Do While (password <> sysPassword)
  Console.Write("Enter your password: ")
  password = Console.ReadLine
Loop
```

Writing code this way, we have to prompt the user to enter a password twice. A better way to do this to use a Do...Loop While statement, like this:

```
Do
  Console.Write("Enter your password: ")
  Password = Console.ReadLine
Loop While (password <> sysPassword)
```

The Do Until Statement

The *Do Until* statement is used when you want to express the idea that the loop should run "until" the test expression becomes True. The general form of the Do Until statement is

```
Do Until (expression)
  Statement body
Loop
```

Some problems are best written using a Do Until statement. Let's look at a variation of the city growth problem. Instead of determining the population growth after a certain number of years, let's write a program that determines when the population of the city will reach half a million people, given a 3% growth rate again:

```
Imports System
Module Loops
  Sub Main()
    Dim growth As Single = 1.03
    Dim population As Single = 150000
    Dim numYears, start As Integer
    start = 1
```

```
Do Until (population >= 500000)
  population *= growth
  start += 1
Loop
Console.WriteLine("The population will reach _
                500,000 in " & start & " years.")
  End Sub
End Module
```

The Do. . .Loop Until Statement

The *Do. . .Loop Until* statement puts the test expression at the bottom of the loop, just as the Do. . .Loop While statement did. The general form of the statement is

```
Do
  Statement body
Loop Until (expression)
```

We can rewrite the password-checking code fragment using the Do. . .Loop Until statement like this:

```
Do
  Console.Write("Enter your password: ")
  password = Console.ReadLine
Loop Until (password = sysPassword)
```

You can substitute a Do While–type loop with a Do Until–type loop in just about any situation. The type of loop you use should be guided by which logic for the test expression is the clearest or easiest to express.

The For Statement

The While and Do statements are used when you want to execute a series of statements while a test expression is True or until the expression becomes True. There are many situations in programming, however, when you want a loop to run a specific number of times. A prime example of such a situation is when you want to perform an operation on every element of an array. The statement you should use in this type of situation is the *For* statement.

The general form of the For statement is

```
For counter-variable = val1 To val2 Step n
   Statement body
Next
```

where *counter-variable* is an Integer variable that assumes values from *val1* to *val2*. *Step n* is an optional increment that, if left out, defaults to 1.

The next program demonstrates one way to use a For statement. The array grades stores a set of student test grades. The program accesses each grade in the array, adding 5 points to the grade. Finally, another For statement is used to display each element in the array. Here's the code:

```
Imports System
Module Grades
   Sub Main()
      Dim grades() As Integer = {83, 73, 90, 100, 62}
      Dim element As Integer
      For element = 0 To grades.GetUpperBound(0)
         If (grades(element) <> 100) Then
            grades(element) += 5
         End If
      Next
      For element = 0 to grades.GetUpperBound(0)
         Console.Write(grades(element) & " ")
      Next
   End Sub
End Module
```

The optional Step clause can be used to change the default increment. Here's an example that sums the odd integers from 1 to 100:

```
Imports System
Module OddInts
   Sub Main()
      Dim int, sum As Integer
      For int = 1 to 100 Step 2
         sum += int
      Next
```

```
      Console.WriteLine("The sum of the first 100 odd _
                        integers is: " & sum)
   End Sub
End Module
```

You can also specify a negative increment in a For statement. The following program displays the elements of an array in reverse order by starting at the last element and moving backward through the array:

```
Imports System
Module Reverse
   Sub Main()
      Dim chars() As Char = {"a"c, "b"c, "c"c, "d"c, "e"c}
      Dim pos As Integer
      For pos = chars.GetUpperBound(0) To 0 Step -1
        Console.Write(chars(pos) & " ")
      Next
   End Sub
End Module
```

If you don't specify a negative number in a decrementing For statement, you won't get an error. The program will execute the statement body one time and then exit the For statement.

For the last example of using For loops, we look at processing a two-dimensional array. This array stores a set of grades for several sections of the same course. The program calculates the average grade for each section, displaying the section number and the average. The program is as follows:

```
Module Module1

   Sub Main()
      Dim grades(,) As Integer = {{72, 83, 67}, {92, 74, _
                                  86}, {100, 84, 93}}
      Dim average As Single
      Dim row, col, endrow, endcol, total As Integer
      endrow = grades.GetUpperBound(0)
      endcol = grades.GetUpperBound(1)
      For row = 0 To endrow
        total = 0
```

```
      For col = 0 To endcol
        total += grades(row, col)
      Next
      average = total / grades.GetLength(1)
      Console.WriteLine("The average for section " & _
                        row + 1 & " is " & average)
    Next
    Console.Write("Press enter to quit")
    Console.Read()
  End Sub

End Module
```

Notice how the length of a column is calculated using the GetLength method of the Array class. The value 1 is passed as an argument because the column is dimension 1 of the array, whereas the row is dimension 0. The same technique is used to return the upper bound of a dimension using the GetUpperBound method.

This example also demonstrates a valuable time-saving technique. You probably noticed that the row and column upper bound values were stored in variables before beginning the nested For statements. This minimizes the number of times the System has to calculate those values. For small arrays, the time saved is not all that great, but for large arrays the time saved can be significant. It is a good idea to get in the habit of using this technique for all sizes of arrays.

The For Each Statement

In the examples in the previous section, a For statement was used to iterate through an array, moving from the 0th element to the last element. An alternative method for accessing the elements of an array (or any other collection-type data structure in VB.NET) is to use the *For Each* statement. This statement accesses every element of a data collection, pulling the element out of the collection and storing it in a variable, giving the program access to the element value.

The general form of the For Each statement is

```
For Each variable In coll
  Statement body
Next
```

where *variable* is a variable of the data type of the elements in the collection, and *coll* is a named collection type, such as an array or a collection.

For Each statements are typically used when you want to perform an operation with or to every element of a data collection. Here is a program that accesses an array of grades for the purposes of calculating the average grade:

```
Imports System
Module Grades
  Sub Main()
    Dim grades() As Integer = {83, 73, 90, 100, 62}
    Dim total, grade As Integer
    Dim average As single
    For Each grade In grades
      total += grade
    Next
    average = total / grades.Length()
    Console.WriteLine("The grade average is: " & _
                    average)
  End Sub
End Module
```

The operation performed by the For Each statement is called an *enumeration*. All well-behaved collections in VB.NET are written to allow enumerations via the For Each statement. Later in the book we will build our own collection classes that include code to allow them to be enumerated with For Each statements.

Writing Subprograms

A first layer of abstraction in a computer program consists of the subprograms you create. Subprograms modularize your code, allowing you to reuse subprograms in other programs and making your programs easier to read and debug. In this section we'll review how to create the two types of subprograms allowed in VB.NET—functions and subroutines.

Functions

A function is a subprogram that returns a value to the calling program. Functions in VB.NET are declared outside of Sub Main() using the following form:

```
Function Function-name(argument-list) As Data-type
   Function-definition
   Return expression
End Function
```

A function is called by writing the function name and its arguments wherever an expression can be placed. The following program, which uses a function to square a number, demonstrates both how to define a function and how a function is called:

```
Imports System
Module Square
   Sub Main()
      Dim num As Integer = 12
      Dim squareNum As Integer
      squareNum = square(num)
      Console.WriteLine(num & " squared is " & squareNum)
   End Sub
   Function square(n As Integer) As Integer
      Return n * n
   End Function

End Module
```

It is important that the data types of the arguments and the function's return value match the function definition or an exception will be thrown.

Arguments to functions are passed by value if you don't specify otherwise. To pass arguments by reference to a function, add the ByRef keyword to the argument in the argument list. In the following program, the square function not only squares the argument passed to it but also permanently changes the argument's value to its square:

```
Imports System
Module Square
   Sub Main()
      Dim num As Integer = 12
      Dim squareNum As Integer
      Console.Write(num)
      squareNum = square(num)
      Console.WriteLine(" squared is " & squareNum)
```

```
    Console.WriteLine("The value of num now is " & num)
  End Sub

  Function square(ByRef n As Integer) As Integer
    n = n * n
    Return n
  End Function

End Module
```

Because we used an assignment statement in the function definition, the value num is permanently changed to the square of its previous value.

Subroutines

Subroutines differ from functions in that a subroutine does not return a value to the calling program. The general form of a subroutine is

```
Sub Subroutine-name(argument-list)
  Subroutine definition
End Sub
```

Subroutines are used most often to perform frequent tasks that take several lines of code to write. For example, in a Windows application, a subroutine is written to clear the textboxes on a form:

```
Sub ClearText()
  txtFirstName.Text = ""
  txtMiddleName.Text = ""
  txtLastName.Text = ""
  txtAddress.Text = ""
  txtCity.Text = ""
  txtState.Text = ""
  txtZipCode.Text = ""
End Sub
```

Less frequently, subroutines are written to perform more complex computational tasks. The following program uses a subroutine to swap two values in the calling program:

```
Imports System
Module Swap
  Sub Main()
    Dim value1, value2 As Integer
    value1 = 12
    value2 = 24
    Console.WriteLine("The value of value1 is: " & _
                       value1)
    Console.WriteLine("The value of value2 is: " & _
                       value2)
    swap(value1, value2)
    Console.WriteLine("After the swap - ")
    Console.WriteLine("The value of value1 is: " _
                       value1)
    Console.WriteLine("The value of value2 is: " _
                       value2)
  End Sub

  Sub swap(ByRef v1 As Integer, ByRef v2 As Integer)
    Dim temp As Integer
    temp = v1
    v1 = v2
    v2 = temp
  End Sub

End Module
```

Subprograms Using Varying and/or Optional Parameters

Subprograms can be written both with a variable number of parameters and with optional parameters that do not have to be present in every call. You should utilize these features when necessary to make your subprograms more powerful and flexible.

A function or subroutine can receive a varying number of arguments by specifying that the argument list be a *parameter array*. A parameter array is denoted by the ParamArray keyword before the array name is given in the parameter list. Parameter arrays must always be passed by value; otherwise the array is treated just like any other array being used as a subprogram parameter.

Parameter arrays are typically used in functions that must sum a set of values and return the total. The following short program illustrates this use of the parameter array:

```
Module Module1

  Sub Main()
    Dim g1, g2, g3, g4 As Integer
    Dim sum1, sum2 As Integer
    g1 = 100
    g2 = 95
    g3 = 90
    g4 = 85
    sum1 = SumGrades(g1, g2)
    sum2 = SumGrades(g1, g2, g3, g4)
    Console.WriteLine("The first sum equals " & sum1)
    Console.WriteLine("The second sum equals " & sum2)
    Console.Write("Press enter to quit")
    Console.Read()
  End Sub

  Function SumGrades(ByVal ParamArray grades() _
                     As Integer) As Integer
    Dim x, total, endGrades As Integer
    endGrades = grades.GetUpperBound(0)
    For x = 0 To endGrades
      total += grades(x)
    Next
    Return total
  End Function

End Module
```

By using a parameter array, the SumGrades function can accept any number of grades. The first call to the function passes two grades; the second call passes four grades. Giving the function this type of flexibility adds considerable power to subprograms in VB.NET.

Another useful subprogram method is to allow a function or subroutine to have optional parameters. An optional parameter is a parameter that is either explicitly passed to the subprogram definition or left out completely, in which case the compiler takes a default value for the parameter as specified in the subprogram definition.

An optional parameter is denoted in a subprogram definition with the keyword Optional. The parameter must also have a default value expressed, so that if the parameter is left out as an argument when the subprogram is called, the compiler will have a value to use when the parameter is used in the subprogram definition.

The following program demonstrates a simple use of optional subprogram parameters. PopGrowth is a function that calculates the growth of a population given a certain growth rate. The parameter for the rate of growth is the optional parameter. Here's the code:

```
Module Module1

  Sub Main()
    Dim pop As Integer
    Dim new_pop As Integer
    Console.Write("Enter the current population: ")
    pop = CInt(Console.ReadLine())
    new_pop = PopGrowth(pop, 2.0)
    Console.WriteLine("The new population is " _
                      & new_pop)
    new_pop = PopGrowth(pop)
    Console.WriteLine("The new population is " _
                      & new_pop)
    Console.Write("Press enter to quit")
    Console.Read()
  End Sub

  Function PopGrowth(ByVal initPop As Integer, _
                    Optional ByVal rate As _
                    Single = 1.0)
    Return initPop * rate
  End Function

End Module
```

In the first call to PopGrowth, both arguments are provided, so the function uses the second argument, 2.0, as the rate of growth for the calculation. In the second call to PopGrowth, just the initial population is provided, so the function uses the default value, 1.0, for the second parameter.

Named Parameters

When a function or subroutine is called, you almost always pass arguments to the subprogram in the same order in which the parameters are listed in the subprogram definition. There are situations, however, when you want to change the order in which arguments are passed to the subprogram call. *Named parameters* allow you to do this.

Naming parameters involves providing the parameter name along with the argument value in a subprogram call. Here's an example using the PopGrowth function from the previous section:

```
Module Module1

   Sub Main()
      Dim pop As Integer
      Dim new_pop As Integer
      Console.Write("Enter the current population: ")
      pop = CInt(Console.ReadLine())
      new_pop = PopGrowth(rate:=1.5, initPop:=pop)
      Console.WriteLine("The new population is " _
                        & new_pop)
      Console.Write("Press enter to quit")
      Console.Read()
   End Sub

   Function PopGrowth(ByVal initPop As Integer, _
                      ByVal rate As Single)
      Return initPop * rate
   End Function

End Module
```

In the call to PopGrowth, the order of the parameters is reversed in the function call, but this is acceptable because each parameter is named. Normally, the compiler matches the order of the parameter with the corresponding argument, but when you use named parameters the compiler doesn't have to match them.

Using named parameters also makes working with optional parameters clearer. Look at the PopGrowth function from the previous section. Here's the function definition again:

```
Function PopGrowth(ByVal initPop As Integer, Optional _
                   ByVal rate As Single = 1.0)
   Return initPop * rate
End Function
```

When the function is called with just one argument, determining exactly which parameter is being addressed can be confusing. When you use named parameters, however, it is very clear which parameter(s) are being addressed:

```
new_pop = PopGrowth(pop := 10000)
```

Recursion

Recursion is both a programming technique and a problem-solving strategy. A recursive function is one that calls itself as part of its definition. VB.NET supports recursion for both subroutines and functions, and there are situations where recursions can be used with both types of subprograms. In this section we'll cover some very basic recursive procedures to demonstrate how to use recursion.

Before we discuss how to write a recursive procedure, let's look at an example. The following program, using a recursive function, calculates a number raised to a power:

```
Module Module1

  Sub Main()
    Dim num, e As Integer
    num = 2
    e = 4
    Console.WriteLine(num & " raised to the " & e & _
                      " power " & " equals " & _
                      power(num, e))
    Console.Write("Press enter to quit")
    Console.Read()
  End Sub

  Function power(ByVal base As Integer, ByVal exp As _
                Integer)
    If (exp = 0) Then
      Return 1
    Else
      Return base * power(base, exp -1)
    End If
  End Function
End Module
```

We'll use the power function written here to explain how recursive procedures work. The strategy followed by all recursive procedures is to continually break a problem down to a simpler problem until the simplest, or most trivial, problem remains. In a problem such as raising a number to a power, you can visualize the problem in the following way: 2^4 would be

```
2 × 2 × 2 × 2 × 1
```

The trivial case, also called the *base case*, returns 1. The base case is coded in the first two lines of the function. The If statement tests to see if the value of exp is equal to 1. If so, the function returns the value 1. Otherwise, the function returns the value of the base (2 in our example) times another call to the function.

What the compiler does, when computing a recursive function, is postpone a series of computations until the base case is reached. The process can be visualized like this:

```
2 × power(2,3)
2 × 2 × power(2,2)
2 × 2 × 2 × power(2,1)
2 × 2 × 2 × 2 × power(2,0)
2 × 2 × 2 × 2 × 1
```

Once the base case is reached, the compiler then works its way back through the postponed computations, like this:

```
2 × 2 × 2 × 2
2 × 2 × 4
2 × 8
16
```

We can understand the concept of recursion better by looking at another example. The factorial of an integer is defined as follows:

```
0! = 1
n! = n × (n-1)!
```

As you can see, this is a recursive definition. The first line, $0! = 1$, is the base case. The next line is a recursion that says multiply n by the factorial of the number that is one less than n. We can translate this into a factorial function quite easily. Here's the code:

```
Function factorial(ByVal n As Integer)
  If (n = 0) Then
    Return 1
  Else
    Return n * factorial(n - 1)
  End If
End Function
```

Given the value 5 passed to the function, we can view the computational process of this function as

```
5 × factorial(4)
5 × 4 × factorial(3)
5 × 4 × 3 × factorial(2)
5 × 4 × 3 × 2 × factorial(1)
5 × 4 × 3 × 2 × 1 × factorial(0)
5 × 4 × 3 × 2 × 1 × 1
5 × 4 × 3 × 2 × 1
5 × 4 × 3 × 2
5 × 4 × 6
5 × 24
120
```

Recursion can be used to solve many types of problems that aren't numerical. As a last example (though one you probably won't want to use in a real program), we'll display the elements of an array using recursion. We display the program first and then provide an explanation. (Note that this program was written with the command-compiler, and not with Visual Studio.NET, which explains why all the keywords are in lowercase.)

```
imports system
module Recurarray
  sub main
    dim nums() as integer = {1,2,3,4,5,6,7,8,9,10}
    PrintArray(nums, 0, nums.getupperbound(0))
  end sub

  sub PrintArray(ar() as integer, first as integer, _
              last as integer)
    if (first > last) then
```

```
      exit sub
    else
      console.write(ar(first) & " ")
      PrintArray(ar, first+1, last)
    end if
  end sub
end module
```

The PrintArray subroutine has three parameters: the array to display, an integer that stores the first index number first, and an integer that stores the upper bound of the array last. The base case compares the value of first to the value of last. If first is greater than last, then the end of the array has been reached and the subroutine should exit. Otherwise, the current array element is displayed and a recursive call to the function is made with the value of the parameter first incremented by 1.

Summary

This chapter presents a whirlwind tour of the primary features of the VB.NET language. Obviously, we can't cover all the features of the language in just one chapter. Nonetheless, the overview of the language provided here should be enough to make a programmer experienced in another language comfortable with reading the rest of the material in this book.

Exercises

1. Write a program that prompts the user to enter three test scores and then displays the user's test score average.
2. Write a program that displays the following:

```
*   *   *   *   *
  *   *   *   *
    *   *   *
      *   *
        *
```

3. Write a program that converts temperatures from either Celsius to Fahrenheit or from Fahrenheit to Celsius. The user should enter a temperature followed by a letter to signify which way to convert the temperature. The program should then display the converted temperature. For example, if

the user enters

```
100 c
```

The program will output

```
212 f
```

Use the Internet to find the formulas for converting temperatures between Celsius and Fahrenheit.

4. Using a For Next loop, write a program that sums the integers 1–100. Rewrite the program using a Do . . . While loop.

5. Write a program that stores a list of school subjects into an array. Using a For Each loop, display the contents of the array 1 subject to a line. Write a third program, a Windows application, that displays the subjects in a list box when the user clicks a button.

6. Write a program that uses a two-dimensional array to keep track of the test scores in a classroom. Use an initialization list to load the array. The program should display the average grade for each student and a total class average. Each row of the array represents one student.

7. Write a Boolean function that returns True if a number is even and False if the number is odd. Use the function in a program.

8. Write a string function that returns the reverse of any string given to it as an argument. Use the function in a program.

9. Write a Double function that calculates the future population of a city if the city's current population is 50,000 and the growth rate is 5 percent a year.

10. Write a subroutine that prints the following banner when called:

```
*************************
*      Hello, world!      *
*************************
```

Use the subroutine in a program.

11. Write a subroutine that will clear all the textboxes on a Windows form. Use the subroutine in a Windows application of your choosing.

12. Using recursion, write a function that determines if the string given to the function is a palindrome. A palindrome is a word that is spelled the same both forward and backward. For example, "bob" is a palindrome.

13. Write a subroutine that swaps the values of two variables. (Hint: You will have to pass the arguments by reference to make this work properly.)

CHAPTER 2

An Overview of Object-Oriented Programming

Object-oriented programming (OOP) is just one in a series of technologies that has been deemed as the savior of software. In the world of computing, software often gets a bad reputation because so many programs are delivered to the end user late, with significant bugs, and not designed to completely solve the problem the program was written to solve. Object-oriented programming provides a set of tools and techniques to help programmers manage program complexity.

OOP DEFINED

Object-oriented programming is a programming technique that involves structuring a program around special, user-defined data types called classes. Classes are used to break a problem up into a set of objects that interact with each other. A class consists of both the data that define an object and subprograms, called methods, which describe the object's behavior.

A language that is to be called a true OOP language must implement three concepts—encapsulation, polymorphism, and inheritance. Without all three of these features, a programming language can be considered object-based, as

Visual Basic 6 is, but all three must be present for the language to be considered a true object-oriented language.

Encapsulation

In the traditional, third-generation programming language (such as earlier versions of Basic, C, and Fortran), all programs consist of two primary elements—program statements and data. The program statements are used to perform operations on the data, but the two elements are always considered to be separate parts of a computer program.

As you'll see later in the chapter, the separation of program code and data can very easily lead to bug-laden programs. When the data and the program are completely independent of each other, it is easy for the data to be changed in ways that the programmer does not intend.

Encapsulation is a mechanism for maintaining a strict separation between program code and data. An OOP language enforces encapsulation by storing data inside an object, along with the subprograms that can transform the data. When designing an object, the designer has the option to make the data and the subprograms public or private. *Public* elements of an object can be accessed by other parts of the program, whereas *private* elements can only be referenced from within the object. Normally, the data elements of an object are kept private while subprograms that allow controlled access to the data a are made public.

Polymorphism

Polymorphism (meaning "many forms") is the ability of one program element to be used in many different situations. Typically, in a traditional computer programming language, this cannot be done. Look at the following function definition:

```
Function Square(num As Integer) As Integer
   Return num * num
End Function
```

This function only works if the argument to the function is an integer. If the program tries to pass a number of a different data type, the compiler complains with a data mismatch error. In an OOP language, one object can have many different methods with the same name that define the same behavior. The ability to have multiple methods with the same name is called *method overloading*.

Method overloading, although useful for designing objects, comes in especially handy for the user of the object. Once the user learns how to use one overloaded method, he or she then knows how to use all the methods. Using the previous example, once the user knows how to square an integer, he or she can square a floating-point number or a long integer.

Inheritance

Objects in an object-oriented language are organized into a hierarchical structure, with more general objects at the top of the structure and more specific instances of the objects at the lower levels of the structure. The more general objects share their behaviors and their data using a mechanism called *inheritance*.

Inheritance is an important tool in managing the complexity of a program. For example, if you are creating a graphics program, you can design an object called Shape that defines what a shape is. You can then define a more specific object, Square, that inherits all the features of Shape, plus adds its own features for defining the attributes and behavior of a square.

If a language doesn't provide inheritance, then each object would have to be completely defined, even if it shared many features with other objects. This leads to much redundant code, makes managing an application more complex, and can also lead to errors in design and coding.

THE CHARACTERISTICS OF AN OOP LANGUAGE

Alan Kay, who is sometimes called the "father" of OOP because of his involvement in the development of the Smalltalk language (considered to be the first truly OOP language), wrote a seminal paper in which he laid out the major characteristics of an OOP language (Kay 1993). Each of these features must be found in a language for it to be considered object-oriented. Let's look at each characteristic in turn to get an understanding of what an OOP language is and how it differs from a more standard programming language.

Everything Is an Object

A properly object-oriented programming language consists of nothing but objects. A better way to put this is to say that every single feature of the language is implemented as a class object.

What does this mean? It means that each feature of the language, from data types to data structures, is an object instance that is inherited from a class or some other object type. You can look at two examples from VB.NET's primitive data types to see that this is true.

When you declare a variable to be of String type, you are actually creating an instance of a String object because the String type is implemented as a class. How can you tell? One way is by how String functions are now called in VB.NET. If we want to determine the length of a string, we call the Length method rather than the Visual Basic 6 len function. Here's how it was done in Visual Basic 6:

```
Dim name As String
name = "Mike McMillan"
Text1.Text = "The length of" & name & " is: " & _
             len(name)
```

Here's how we do it in VB.NET:

```
Dim name As New String("Mike McMillan")
Console.WriteLine("The length of " name & " is: " & _
                  name.Length())
```

There are two major differences here. In the first line, the variable name is assigned the string value "Mike McMillan," but there is no assignment operator used. In OOP, objects are created using something called a constructor. The constructor is responsible for associating the value passed to it with the object that is calling the constructor. We will talk more about constructors in Chapter 3.

In the second line, rather than pass the string variable to a function, the function is called with the variable name and the dot operator. This is an example of message-passing, which is actually one of the other characteristics of an object-oriented language, so we'll explain what this means later in this section. For now, just be aware that objects in an OOP language call their methods (functions) instead of being passed to them.

The String class, along with all the other data types in VB.NET, is derived from the System.Object class. We explain what a derived class is later in the book; for now, we can say that a derived class uses inheritance to obtain some, most, or all of its functionality from another class, called the base class. Most, if not all, entities in VB.NET are inherited from the System.Object class.

The example cited here demonstrates how the features of VB.NET are object-oriented. Equally important for understanding that everything must be an object is for the programmer to think of the problems he or she is solving in terms of objects. If I am going to write a program to keep track of student grades, I naturally think of the student as the primary object in the problem.

When a problem is broken down into objects, the objects must be defined in terms of what they represent (the data) and their behavior (how they transform the data). For example, a student object will need a name, an identification number, a major, a list of courses currently being taken, the current grade for each course, demographic data such as address and phone number, and so on.

The behaviors are less obvious in this example, but we can include the means for computing the student's grade point average or for displaying his or her list of courses and grades, among other behaviors. Behaviors are defined in an object-oriented language using functions, which in OOP parlance are called *methods*.

Computation by Message-Passing

The second feature of an OOP language is that the primary means of computation is through intercommunications between objects. The term used to describe this is *message-passing*.

Computation is performed in an object-oriented language by objects passing messages to each other. Messages are sent to an object via the methods defined for the object. If I want to assign a grade to a course for a Student object, there must be a method that defines how the grade is to be assigned. The message will often include data that the method needs to complete its task. For example, a grade-setting message to a Student object might include both the name of the course and the grade.

Another important feature of OOP related to message-passing is the concept of *information hiding*. The idea behind information hiding is that the sender of a message does not need to know how the method receiving the message does its work. All the sender has to be responsible for is calling the right method and knowing which data (arguments) have to be passed to the method, if any. It is the responsibility of the designer of the object's method to make sure it performs its computation correctly.

The concept of information hiding resembles the black box theory of function design. In electronics, one often encounters such "black boxes." Consider a cable converter. You don't have to know how the cable converter works; you just have to know where to plug the inputs to the box and where to plug the output from the box. Similarly, the user of a function doesn't have to understand how a function computes its output as long as the inputs and the desired outputs are known.

Although methods and functions share the concept of information hiding, that is really where the similarities end. A method is tied to a particular object whereas a function is tied only to the program where it is defined and used. Also, object methods can have varying behavior based on the object that calls the method. For example, a Print method for a Name object might print a name all on one line, whereas a Print method for an Address object might print the address on separate lines. The ability to have one method definition with different behaviors is called overloading, and we discuss this technique in depth later in the book (see Chapter 4).

Objects Store Their Own Data

In a traditional program, variables store the data used for computation. Even though the variables might be global or local to a function or even a construct (like a For loop), the data are still available to any other entity sharing that part of the program. Storing data in the object is part of the concept of encapsulation.

Objects in an object-oriented language store their own data. This feature provides the designer of the object with the ability to protect access to the data. Data protection prohibits illegal or unintended use of the data stored in the object. Why? Because storing data in an object is performed by a method and not by direct assignment.

Let's look at an example. The following short code fragment declares an Integer value and initializes the value to an integer value:

```
Dim salary As Integer = 30000
```

When a value is stored in a simple variable, the only restriction on the value stored in the variable is that the value be within the restrictions of the data type. The following assignments are acceptable for this data type, even though they don't make sense for the semantic value of the variable:

```
salary = 1000000  ' Probably not
salary = 1        ' Hope not
```

Because a class object's data are assigned with methods, you can write code to validate data assignments:

```
If (tempSalary < 5000 Or tempSalary > 100000) Then
  salary = tempSalary
Else
  Console.Write("Salary out of range.)
End if
```

Objects as Class Instances

All of the objects in an object-oriented program are created as instances of a particular class. An instance is a variable declared as a class type. For example, if I have a Person class and declare a variable named myWife that is of Person type (class), then myWife is an instance of the Person class. Any class object that stores data and behavior has to be declared as an instance of the class. There can be classes that don't have instances (think of the Console class that is used to work with data entered and/or displayed on the display), but any object that is required to store data and perform operations on these data must be declared as an instance.

Objects of the Same Type Behave Alike

A class definition specifies the data and behaviors that every instance of the class will exhibit. If I define a TimeStamp class that automatically stores the System time whenever a new TimeStamp object is created, every instance of the class will perform this behavior.

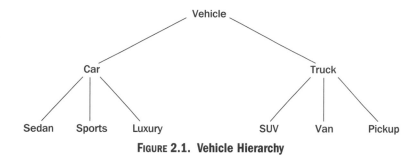

FIGURE 2.1. Vehicle Hierarchy

One of the successes of OOP as a tool for code reuse is that, once a class is created, any programmer using the class can know exactly how that class is going to behave every time an instance of the class is used. Imagine how confusing it would it be if the Display behavior of a Name class sometimes printed the name in first name, last name order and sometimes in last name, first name order.

Objects Are Organized into Hierarchies

All object-oriented systems (languages and programs) are organized into a hierarchy of objects. The objects that make up the VB.NET System are based primarily on the System.Object class. Each object, be it a data type, a Windows form, or a control used on a form, inherits its features from the System.Object class.

A hierarchy of objects starts with one object that is considered the root object. Figure 2.1 illustrates a hierarchy of four-wheeled vehicles.

You can understand how inheritance works by looking at the hierarchy of vehicles. The root object of the hierarchy is vehicle. All vehicles have certain features in common—a steering wheel, an engine, seats, etc. An instance of any vehicle type will have these features.

The next layer down in the hierarchy comprises car and truck. Both of these objects are instances of vehicles, meaning they share, or inherit, all the features of a vehicle, but they also have their own features.

If you move down the car hierarchy there are three different types—sedan, sports, and luxury. Each of these car types shares the features of a car, and of a vehicle, but they each have their own distinctive features.

By organizing our objects into hierarchies, we can take advantage of inheritance to make our programs more efficient and powerful. Once we define the features of a root object, called a base class, we can use these features in objects that inherit from the base class, called derived classes. In other words, we can use the code written in a base class in a derived class without having to write the code again. Several chapters later in the book (especially Chapters 4 and 5) discuss the use of inheritance in great depth.

OOP AS AN ABSTRACTION MECHANISM

Abstraction is a key tool in computer programming. Abstraction is the removing or separating of some aspects of an entity or process to focus on other aspects of an entity or process. A road map, for example, removes details about the terrain of an area to focus on the roads of that area. A topographic map, in contrast, removes details about the roads of an area to focus on the terrain of that area.

In computer programming, abstraction is used in several ways to manage the complexity of a programming problem. At a very high level, the programming language you use is an abstraction of the machine language that the computer's processor has to use to actually do its computation. Computer programming was a slow and tedious task before high-level languages were developed.

At a lower level, the use of functions and subroutines comprises the most common layer of abstraction to most programmers. A function is used to remove the details of code that will potentially be used many times in a program. As an example, look at the following VB.NET program that calculates what day Easter falls on in a given year:

```
Module Module1

  Sub Main()

    Dim year As Integer = 2003
    Dim day As Integer
    Dim a, b, c, d, e As Integer
    a = year Mod 19
    b = year Mod 4
    c = year Mod 7
    d = (19 * a + 24) Mod 30
    e = (2 * b + 4 * c + 6 * d + 5) Mod 7
```

```
      day = 22 + d + e
      If day < 32 Then
        Console.WriteLine("Easter is March " & day & " _
                          in year " & year)
      ElseIf (day > 31) Then
        day = day - 31
        Console.WriteLine("Easter is April " & day & " _
                          in year " & year)
      End If
      year = 2004
      a = year Mod 19
      b = year Mod 4
      c = year Mod 7
      d = (19 * a + 24) Mod 30
      e = (2 * b + 4 * c + 6 * d + 5) Mod 7
      day = 22 + d + e
      If day < 32 Then
        Console.WriteLine("Easter is March " & day & " _
                          in year " & year)
      ElseIf (day > 31) Then
        day = day - 31
        Console.WriteLine("Easter is April " & day & " _
                          in year " & year)
      End If
      End Sub

End Module
```

This code is not that complex, but if you use it many times in a program it will take up space and make your code messy and harder to understand. Here we just use the code twice.

The simple solution to this problem is to remove the Easter calculation code from the main program and put it into a function. Here is the previous program rewritten to use a function:

```
Module Module1

  Sub Main()
    Dim thisYear As Integer = 2002
```

```
      Dim easter As Integer
      easter = EasterCalc(thisYear)
      If (easter < 32) Then
        Console.WriteLine("Easter is on March " & easter)
      ElseIf (easter > 31) Then
        easter = EasterCalc(thisYear)
        easter -= 31
        Console.WriteLine("Easter is on April " & easter)
      End If
      thisYear = 2004
      easter = EasterCalc(thisYear)
      If (easter < 32) Then
        Console.WriteLine("Easter is on March " & easter)
      ElseIf (easter > 31) Then
        easter = EasterCalc(thisYear)
        easter -= 31
        Console.WriteLine("Easter is on April " & easter)
      End If
      Console.Read()
    End Sub
    Function EasterCalc(ByVal year As Integer)
      Dim day As Integer
      Dim a, b, c, d, e As Integer
      a = year Mod 19
      b = year Mod 4
      c = year Mod 7
      d = (19 * a + 24) Mod 30
      e = (2 * b + 4 * c + 6 * d + 5) Mod 7
      day = 22 + d + e
      Return day
    End Function
End Module
```

By putting the code for calculating the date of Easter into a function, we abstract the details of the calculation out of the main program and place them in the function definition. If users of the function don't need or care to know the details of how the calculation is performed, they don't have to look at the function definition. The function can just be used over and over again.

Objects provide the same type of abstraction. When you define the behavior of a class via a set of methods (remember, methods are another name for functions and subroutines in an object-oriented language), the user of the class doesn't have to know any of the details of the methods to use them.

ABSTRACT DATA TYPES

We can carry the concept of abstraction to the design of our programs by using abstract data types. An *abstract data type* (ADT) is a data type that defines both the data of the type and the data operations allowed by the type. An ADT is a user-defined data type that is defined in an implementation-independent way so that the "what" of the ADT is communicated to the programmer, who can then implement the ADT using any programming language he or she chooses. The operations make up the *interface* of the ADT, which specifies how the user of the ADT may work with the data.

An ADT Example

An appointment-tracking computer program needs to keep track of time. For example, the program needs to know exactly how many minutes it is until the next appointment or how much time there is between the first appointment of the day and the last appointment.

To facilitate the design of the program, we create an abstract data type for time, calling it `TimeType`. The `TimeType` ADT keeps track of three data fields: hours, minutes, and seconds. The operations for the ADT include displaying the time, adjusting the time between twelve-hour format and twenty-four-hour format, comparing two times for equality, and performing arithmetic operations on times.

The ADT Format

An ADT definition uses a format that mirrors as much as possible how the ADT will be implemented in code. The format starts with a header that includes the name of the ADT, a description of the data type, and a list of the ADT's operations. Each operation is further defined by the inputs to the data type (data coming from the client), any preconditions necessary before using the

ADT, the process (actions performed with the data), the output of the ADT, and any postconditions (the state of the ADT after executing the operation).

A template showing a generalized ADT format is as follows:

ADT **ADT_Name:**
  Data
    The structure of the data
  Operation(1)

Input:	Data received from the client.
Preconditions:	The required state of the ADT before the operation can be performed.
Process:	Actions performed with data.
Output:	Data returned to the client.
Postconditions:	The resulting state of the ADT after executing the operation.

  Operation(2)
    . . .
  Operation(n)
    . . .
End **ADT_Name**

We can now develop our `TimeType` ADT using this format.

ADT **TimeType:**
  Data
    The hours, minutes, and seconds of the time. Each of these is stored as an Integer. The time is originally stored in 24-hour format, but it can be converted to 12-hour format. The hours number can be in the range from 0 to 23. The minutes number can be in the range from 0 to 59. The seconds number can be in the range from 0 to 59.
  Operations
    Initialize

Input:	None.
Preconditions:	None.
Process:	Set each data member to 0.
Output:	None.
Postconditions:	Each data member is set to 0.

    SetTime

Input:	Hours, minutes, and seconds.

Preconditions: None.

Process: Set each data member to respective integer.

Output: None.

Postconditions: Each data member contains the number assigned to it.

Display

Input: None.

Preconditions: None.

Process: Each data member is tested to see if its value is less than 9. If the value is less than 9, the value has a "0" added to the front of the value and the value is converted to a string.

Output: The time in hh:mm:ss format.

Postconditions: None.

End TimeType

These are not all the operations needed for the TimeType ADT, but these few operations give you an idea of how an ADT is defined. Notice that nowhere in the definition is there any use of actual code. The main purpose of the ADT, again, is to describe what the ADT is and does, not how it is implemented.

Another ADT Example

Let's look at another ADT example. This one is an abstract type for a person's name. A name is made up of at least three parts—first name, middle name, and last name. Some names have other parts, such as Thurston Howell III, and some people have just one name (e.g., Cher), but we'll use only "well-formed" names for this example.

Besides storing the different parts of a name, a Name ADT also must be able to display a name in different ways: first name—middle name—last name; last name, first name, middle initial; or just all initials. We must have operations for each of these name formats.

Here is the Name ADT format:

ADT **Name:**

Data

The data for the ADT consists of the first name, the middle name, and the last name. Each of these data members is stored as a string.

Operations
 SetName
  Input: Strings for first name, middle name, and last name.
  Preconditions: None.
  Process: Set each data member to string value.
  Output: None.
  Postconditions: Data members set to string value.
 Clear
  Input: None.
  Preconditions: None.
  Process: Set data members to empty string.
  Output: None.
  Postconditions: All data members set to empty string.
 showFirstLast
  Input: None.
  Preconditions: None.
  Process: Create string of data members in first name-middle name-last name format. Display string.
  Output: Name in first-middle-last format.
  Postconditions: None.
 showLastFirst
  Input: None.
  Preconditions: None.
  Process: Create string of data members in last name-first name-middle name format. Display string.
  Output: Name in last-first-middle format.
  Postconditions: None.
 showInitials
  Input: None.
  Preconditions: None.
  Process: Extract first character from each data member.
  Output: Initials of name.
  Postconditions: None.
 Copy
  Input: A second Name object.
  Preconditions: None.

Process:	Copy the data members from the current object to the passed-in object.
Output:	None.

     Equal

Input:	A second Name object.
Preconditions:	None.
Process:	Compare the data members of the two Name objects to see if they are all equal.
Output:	True if all data members of both objects are equal; False otherwise.
Postconditions:	None.

End ADT

DESIGNING OBJECT-ORIENTED PROGRAMS

The ADT can be considered a design tool for building object-oriented programs. It is, however, a fairly low level tool that is used once you've determined what objects your program will contain. There are other tools you can use to help you determine how to break a problem into its constituent objects. We examine some of these tools in this section.

CRC Cards

The first step in an object-oriented design (OOD) is to determine the objects of the problem. For each object we have to identify its primary; these primaries then become the building blocks of a class. Once we've identified the properties of a class, we have to define what actions the class is responsible for taking. These responsibilities take the form of messages that are used to interact (collaborate) with other objects.

An object-oriented program will usually be a collection of objects that interact with each other. Each object is responsible for its part of the problem, and combining objects in the proper way leads to a solution to the problem and a design for the program that solves the problem.

To facilitate this process in our OOD, we can use a tool called a CRC card. CRC stands for classes, responsibilities, and collaborations. A CRC card can be an index card, or even just a piece of paper, where you write down all the

Class Name:	Superclasses:	Subclasses:
Responsibilities	Collaborations	

FIGURE 2.2. Sample CRC Card

important characteristics of the objects in your problem solution. A sample CRC card is shown in Figure 2.2.

CRC cards are used to organize the objects used in a program. Each object gets its own card. The class name is written in under Class Name. For now, don't worry about the Superclasses and Subclasses slots. Below the class name come the responsibilities of the object. An object's responsibilities are those tasks the object is expected to perform. The other objects that can be collaborators with the subject object are listed on the right side of the card.

Let's design a sample class to see how this works. To keep track of the grades in a class, a teacher might decide to design a grade book application. One of the objects in the application will be a Student object. So we take a card and write Student as the class name. Next we have to list the responsibilities of the object. The responsibilities of a Student object are to know its name, its student id number, and the courses it is taking. Its collaborators include Course objects and a Grade Book object. The CRC card for the Student object is shown in Figure 2.3.

Class Name: Student	Superclasses:	Subclasses:
Responsibilities	Collaborators	
1. Know name	1. Course	
2. Know id	2. Grade book	
3. Know courses		

FIGURE 2.3. CRC Card for Student Class

From this CRC card we can design an ADT, which can then be used as the basis for an object-oriented program written in VB.NET. Here's the ADT for the Student class:

ADT **Student:**
Data
> The data for the Student class consists of the student's name and the student's id number, which are stored as a string, and a list of the student's course list, which is stored as an array of strings.

Operations
GetName

Input:	None.
Preconditions:	A name must be stored in the field.
Process:	Retrieve name from field.
Output:	The name in first name, last name format.
Postconditions:	None.

SetName

Input:	A name in String format.
Preconditions:	None.
Process:	Input is assigned to Name field.
Output:	None.
Postconditions:	None.

Get ID

Input:	None.
Preconditions:	An id number must be stored in field.
Process:	Retrieve id number from field.
Output:	An id number in string format.
Postconditions:	None.

Set ID

Input:	An id number in string format.
Preconditions:	None.
Process:	Input is assigned to id number field.
Output:	None.
Postconditions:	None.

GetCourses

Input:	None.
Preconditions:	A list of courses must be stored in the array field.
Process:	Iterate through course array, displaying each course.

        Output: A list of courses.
        Postconditions: None.
     SetCourses
          Input: A list of courses in string format.
          Preconditions: None.
          Process: Input is assigned as elements to course array.
          Output: None.
          Postconditions: None.
End ADT

In the next few chapters of this book, you will learn how to take the design for an object-oriented program and turn it into executable code.

SUMMARY

Object-oriented programming is a collection of tools and techniques that are used to manage the complexity inherent in using computer programs to solve real-world problems. The concepts that define OOP include encapsulation, polymorphism, and inheritance. Programs written in an OOP language combine data and subprograms that modify the data into one package called a class. Encapsulating data and operations into a single class (also called an object) allows the programmer greater control over how the data in his or her program are used.

Polymorphism refers to the ability of multiple subprograms written in an OOP language to have the same name. For example, in VB.NET, a function to square a number can have one name but accept arguments in multiple data types. This is not possible in older versions of Visual Basic. Finally, inheritance allows our classes to "inherit" their behavior from more general classes, which means that the subprograms defined for a general class can be used in a more specific (derived) class.

Two methods of designing object-oriented programs are discussed: CRC cards and abstract data types. Both of these methods provide the programmer with the opportunity to think through the creation of a class or set of classes before actually writing the code for them. CRC cards are useful in brainstorming sessions when a programming team fleshes out what objects should be used in a particular problem scenario. CRC cards list the class, the responsibilities (behavior of the class), and any other classes (collaborators) with which the class must interact.

An abstract data type is a more detailed view of the responsibilities of a class. The ADT definition includes a list of the data stored in the class, along with the methods (operations) that define the class's behavior. Detailed information about how each method is supposed to perform is listed along with the inputs to the method and what the method should output. A good programmer should be able to take an ADT specification and write the code for a class.

Design methodologies such as CRC cards and ADTs are important to learn. Experienced programmers always devise some sort of design before they begin coding, even if it's just a quick CRC card and ADT definition. Getting your thoughts together on how your class design should look will keep you from making too many false starts in your program, though it is common to have to start a program design over from scratch at least once.

An excellent introduction to the general concepts of OOP is Timothy Budd's textbook, An Introduction to Object-Oriented Programming. (Budd 2002).

EXERCISES

1. The computer system you are using does not have a built-in data type to store dates. Create a CRC card for a Date class. Using your CRC card design, create an ADT for a Date class.
2. A rational number is a number that can be written in the form *a/b*, where *a* is any integer and *b* is any nonzero integer. Design an ADT for a rational number class. Include behavior for basic arithmetic and displaying a rational number.
3. You need an address book program to help you keep up with your busy social life. Design a CRC card for an address book class and then create an ADT to define the data and the behavior of the class.

CHAPTER 3

Structures

A structure is a user-defined data type that allows a single variable to store more than one type of data. In Visual Basic 6, structures were actually called user-defined types. The structure object has been improved in VB.NET, however, because VB.NET structures can contain both data and subprocedures to operate on those data. Structures are very common in form to classes, though they have several limitations that restrict their use to solve object-oriented programming problems. Because they are similar in form to classes, structures provide an excellent introduction to the use of classes, which is why we spend an entire chapter discussing them.

USING STRUCTURES

In Chapter 2 you were introduced to the concept of the abstract data type. To implement an ADT in VB.NET, we need to use a special data type called a *structure*. A structure allows us to store multiple components of different data types in one logical unit. In some languages structures are known as records.

The atomic data types (Integer, Single, String) allow us to store only single data items in a variable, as does an array (well, not strictly, since an array can be of type Object). For example, when we store a number in an Integer variable, we can only store one number in the variable. With structures, we can store more than one piece of the data in the structure and the data can be of different types. More importantly, a structure allows us to implement data that have "structure," such as a name that is structured as a first name, a middle name, and a last name.

Structures Defined

An ADT is made up of data and operations for working with these data. We can implement an ADT in VB.NET as a structure. Each data component is called a *member*. Every member has a *member name*.

The operations of a structure are called *methods*. Each method has a *method name*. A method is created within a structure as either a function or a subroutine.

Structures are defined in a VB.NET program outside of Sub Main(). Structures can be defined with any of the usual access modifiers, depending on the access level you want to give the structure. The first line of a structure declaration is called the *structure heading*. A typical structure heading is as follows:

```
Public Structure Name
```

A structure is always closed with an ending statement:

```
End Structure
```

After the heading you can declare the members of the structure and the methods. Member declarations usually come before method definitions, but this is not a strict rule. It is just considered good programming style to place all member declarations at the beginning of a structure definition, followed by method definitions.

The list of member declarations at the beginning of a structure definition is called the *member list*. A member declaration looks just like a variable declaration. The Dim keyword is followed by the member name, the As keyword, and the data type of the member. As an example, let's look at the declaration for a structure to keep track of a person's name:

```
Public Structure Name
   Dim FirstName As String
   Dim MiddleName As String
   Dim LastName As String
   . . .
End Structure
```

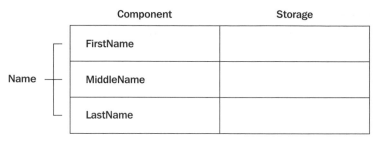

FIGURE 3.1. The Name Structure

Member names must be unique within a structure declaration. The editor will flag an error if you try to declare two members with the same name. When you create a structure definition, you are not using memory. A structure uses memory only when a variable of the structure data type is declared.

To use a structure definition in a program, you must declare a variable to be of the structure type. You use the structure name just like a built-in data type. For example,

```
Dim myName As New Name
Dim yourName As New Name
```

Here myName and yourName are now variables of type Name. Once a structure variable is declared, memory storage is reserved for each of the data members in the structure. For all practical purposes, the structure members are stored in contiguous memory addresses, allowing for efficient retrieval of each member. Figure 3.1 illustrates how a structure is stored in memory.

Accessing Structure Members

Individual structure members are accessed (for assigning and retrieving values) by giving the name of the structure variable, a dot (period), and the member name. This expression is called a *member selector*.

The period that separates the structure variable name from the member name is called the *dot operator*, as you probably already know, since you've already used this operator with many of the .NET Framework classes. The following line shows how to assign a value to the FirstName member of a Name variable:

```
myName.FirstName = "Mike"
```

This example demonstrates assigning a value to a structure member. We can access the value in the member in the same way:

```
Dim fname As String
fname = myName.FirstName
```

Obviously, member selectors can be used in exactly the same way as any other variable we have used previously. We can use them as targets of assignment statements, we can use them as values in assignment statements, we can pass them as arguments to methods, and so on.

The following program demonstrates the use of member selectors. The user's first name, middle name, and last name are retrieved from the keyboard. The Substring method is then used to extract the first letter of each name to display just the user's initials. Here's the code:

```
Dim myName As New Name()
Dim initials As String
Console.Write("Enter your first name: ")
myName.FirstName = Console.ReadLine()
Console.Write("Enter your middle name: ")
myName.MiddleName = Console.ReadLine()
Console.Write("Enter your last name: ")
myName.LastName = Console.ReadLine()
initials = myName.FirstName.Substring(0, 1) & _
           myName.MiddleName.Substring(0, 1) & _
           myName.LastName.Substring(0, 1)
Console.WriteLine("Your initials are " & initials & ".")
Console.Write("Press Enter to quit")
Console.Read()
```

Arrays as Structure Members

A structure member can be any legal VB.NET data type, and a member can be a composite type such as an array. Arrays are common in structures because you often need to store multiple values of a single data item. For example, if we have a structure to keep track of a student's test scores in a class, we can use an array to keep track of all the student's scores in the class.

Using an array in a structure is not too complicated, though there is one area that is likely to trip you up. The following structure definition creates a structure for the scenario just discussed:

```
Public Structure TestScores
   Dim StudentName as String
   Dim Grades() As Integer
End Structure
```

Notice that the array Grades is declared without specifying the actual size of the array. You can't assign a size to the array until you've created an actual structure object. Then, you just use the Redim reserved word to assign the array's size.

The following program demonstrates how to use an array as a structure member:

```
Imports System
Module ArrayMember

   Public Structure TestScores
      Dim StudentName as String
      Dim Grades() As Integer
   End Structure

   Sub Main()
      Dim introProg As TestScores
      Redim introProg.Grades(2)
      introProg.StudentName = "Raymond Williams"
      introProg.Grades(0) = 82
      introProg.Grades(1) = 94
      introProg.Grades(2) = 85
      Dim x, total As Integer
      Dim average As Single
      For x = 0 to introProg.Grades.GetUpperBound(0)
         total += introProg.Grades(x)
      Next
      average = total / introProg.Grades.Length
      Console.WriteLine("Test average for " & _
                     introProg.StudentName & _
                     " is: " & average)
   End Sub

End Module
```

Comparing Structure Objects

Two objects of the same structure type cannot be compared aggregately. They must be compared member-by-member. If we have two Name objects and want to see if they're storing the same name, we must compare for equality the FirstName members of both objects, the MiddleName members of both objects, and the LastName members of both objects. If all three comparisons for equality are true, then the two Name objects have the same member values and are equal.

The following code fragment performs an equality test on two Name objects:

```
If (myName.FirstName = yourName.FirstName) And _
   (myName.MiddleName = yourName.MiddleName) And _
   (myName.LastName = yourName.LastName) Then
  Console.Write("The two names are equal.")
Else
  Console.Write("The two names are not equal.")
End If
```

The following code fragment will result in an error:

```
If (myName = yourName) Then
  Console.Write("The two names are equal.")
Else
  Console.Write("The two names are not equal.")
End If
```

Structure Input/Output

As with comparison operations, no aggregate operations are allowed for structure input and output. Each structure member must be dealt with individually for these operations.

The following code fragment demonstrates how we can use interactive input from the console to enter the members of a Name object:

```
Imports System
Module NameInput

   Public Structure Name
     Dim FirstName As String
```

```
      Dim MiddleName As String
      Dim LastName As String
   End Structure

   Sub Main()

     Dim myName As Name
     Console.Write("Enter your first name: ")
     myName.FirstName = Console.ReadLine()
     Console.Write("Enter your middle name: ")
     myName.MiddleName = Console.ReadLine()
     Console.Write("Enter your last name: ")
     myName.LastName = Console.ReadLine()
     Console.WriteLine("Your name is: " & _
                        myName.FirstName & " " & _
                        myName.MiddleName & " " & _
                        myName.LastName)
    End Sub
 End Module
```

After the user enters all the parts of his or her name, the Name members are accessed and displayed. This line demonstrates how structure member output is performed.

Operations on Structures

There are only a few operations you can perform on structures as a whole. These operations are called *aggregate* operations because the operation works on the total structure, not on the individual components. The legal structure aggregate operations are

- assignment,
- argument passage, and
- return value from a function.

Assignment

When you have two structure objects of the same type, you can assign the values of all the member elements of one object to another object. Structure assignment alleviates the need to assign each element individually, which is very inefficient. The following code fragment demonstrates how to assign one structure object's values to another object:

```
Public Structure Name
   Dim FirstName As String
   Dim MiddleName As String
   Dim LastName As String
End Structure
. . .
Dim myName as New Name
Dim yourName As New Name
myName.FirstName = "Raymond"
myName.MiddleName = "Gene"
myName.LastName = "Williams"
yourName = myName
```

After the assignment statement, both Name objects hold the same values for each of the data members. This operation is much more efficient than if each data member had to be assigned individually:

```
yourName.FirstName = myName.FirstName
yourName.MiddleName = myName.MiddleName
yourName.LastName = myName.LastName
```

Passing a Structure as an Argument to a Subprogram

A structure can be passed to a subprogram. A structure is a value data type, so if you want to make permanent changes to the structure in a function or a subroutine, you must pass the structure by reference. The following program illustrates the mechanics of passing structures to subprograms.

There are two subroutines in the program, ChangeFirst and ChangeFirst1. ChangeFirst accepts the structure passed to it by the calling program by value, so that even though the code in the subroutine changes the first name of the structure passed to it, when the structure is accessed in Sub Main(), the original value of FirstName is displayed.

ChangeFirst1, in contrast, accepts the structure by reference, so that when the subroutine changes the value of the first name, the change is reflected when the structure member FirstName is displayed in Sub Main(). Here's the code:

```
Imports System
Module NameStructure

  Public Structure Name
    Dim FirstName As String
    Dim MiddleName As String
    Dim LastName As String
  End Structure

  Sub Main()
    Dim myName As Name
    myName.FirstName = "Michael"
    myName.MiddleName = "Mason"
    myName.LastName = "McMillan"
    ChangeFirst(myName)
    Console.WriteLine(myName.FirstName & " " & _
                      myName.MiddleName & _
                      " " & myName.LastName)
    ChangeFirst1(myName)
    Console.WriteLine(myName.FirstName & " " & _
                      myName.MiddleName & _
                      " " & myName.LastName)
  End Sub

  Sub ChangeFirst(ByVal aName As Name)
    aName.FirstName = "Steven"
  End Sub

  Sub ChangeFirst1(ByRef aName As Name)
    aName.FirstName = "Steven"
  End Sub
End Module
```

The output from this program is

```
Michael Mason McMillan
Steven Mason McMillan
```

If a structure is not passed to a subprogram explicitly by reference, the changes made to the structure in the subprogram are actually affecting the copy of the structure passed to the subprogram and not the structure itself.

Structures as Subprogram Return Values

A structure can be passed as the return value of a function. Because the return value is actually passed to the calling program, it doesn't matter if you pass a structure into the function by reference or by value. Either way will work.

The following example passes a structure to a function, copies the members of the structure to a temporary structure object, and then returns a structure to be assigned to a new structure object in the calling program:

```
Imports System
Module NameInput

   Public Structure Name
      Dim FirstName As String
      Dim MiddleName As String
      Dim LastName As String
   End Structure

   Sub Main()

      Dim myName As Name
      Dim yourName As Name
      Dim initials As String
      myName.FirstName = "Michael"
      myName.MiddleName = "Mason"
      myName.LastName = "McMillan"
      yourName = CopyName(myName)
      Console.WriteLine("The value of yourName is: ")
      Console.Write(yourName.FirstName & " " & _
                  yourName.MiddleName & _
                  " " & yourName.LastName)

   End Sub

   Function CopyName(ByRef aName As Name) As Name
      Dim tempName As Name
      tempName.FirstName = aName.FirstName
      tempName.MiddleName = aName.MiddleName
      tempName.LastName = aName.LastName
```

```
      Return tempName
   End Function

End Module
```

Structure Arrays

A program that tracks the student grades of a test might use a structure to store each student's data. The structure is made up of the student's name, ID number, and grade on the test. The structure definition looks like this:

```
Public Structure Student
   Dim Name As String
   Dim ID As String
   Dim Grade As Integer
End Structure
```

Because a class will have more than one student, we need to store many student records in our program. To do this, we need an array. We can create an array of Student type just like we can create an array of any of the built-in types.

```
Dim StudentRec(19) As Student
```

This statement creates an array named StudentRec that has memory allocated for 20 Student objects. Each element of the array is of Student type. The diagram in Figure 3.2 illustrates how one element of the array is stored.

To demonstrate how an array of a structure type can be used, let's continue the example of storing student grades on a test by writing the code to store a set of five grades in the array and determine the average grade. Here's the program:

```
Imports System
Module StudentGrades

   Public Structure Student
      Dim Name As String
      Dim ID As String
      Dim Grade As Integer
   End Structure
```

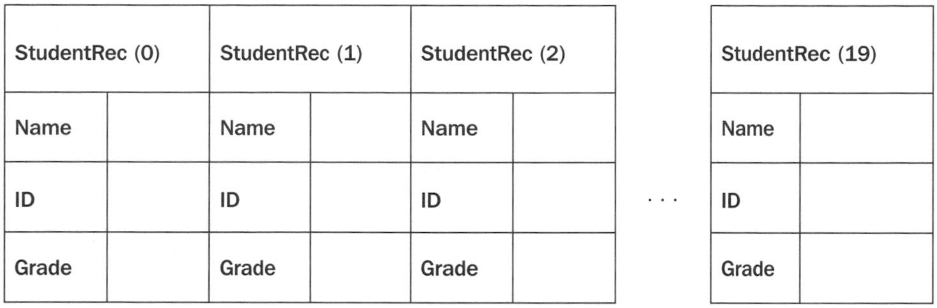

StudentRec (0)		StudentRec (1)		StudentRec (2)			StudentRec (19)	
Name		Name		Name			Name	
ID		ID		ID		⋯	ID	
Grade		Grade		Grade			Grade	

FIGURE 3.2. **Array of Student Records**

```
Sub Main()

   Dim StudentRec(4) As Student
   StudentRec(0).Name = "Carissa Summerhill"
   StudentRec(0).ID = "00001"
   StudentRec(0).Grade = 83
   StudentRec(1).Name = "Ken Cates"
   StudentRec(1).ID = "00023"
   StudentRec(1).Grade = 100
   StudentRec(2).Name = "Matt Hoffman"
   StudentRec(2).ID = "01111"
   StudentRec(2).Grade = 73
   StudentRec(3).Name = "Shalimar Jones"
   StudentRec(3).ID = "00002"
   StudentRec(3).Grade = 82
   StudentRec(4).Name = "Ken Chen"
   StudentRec(4).ID = "10000"
   StudentRec(4).Grade = 65

   Dim x, total As Integer
   Dim average As Single
   For x = 0 to StudentRec.GetUpperBound(0)
      total = total + StudentRec(x).Grade
   Next x
   average = total / StudentRec.Length()
   Console.WriteLine("The average for the class is: " _
                  & average)

   End Sub
End Module
```

The output from this program is

```
The average for the class is: 80.6
```

Structures Composed of Structures

You can build more complex structures by including a structure as the member of a structure. Continuing with the student test score example, let's create a much more complex student record.

First, we'll extend the information we store about the student. We can use the Name structure to include the student's complete name. We'll include the student's ID number, and we'll also store the student's class rank. We will create a structure for the student's permanent home address that includes their street address, city, state, and zip code.

You start a complex structure definition by defining the structures that are considered substructures of the major structure. The definitions for the example in this section are as follows:

```
Public Structure Name
   Dim FirstName As String
   Dim MiddleName As String
   Dim LastName As String
End Structure

Public Structure Address
   Dim Street As String
   Dim City As String
   Dim State As String
   Dim Zip As String
End Structure

Public Structure Student
   Dim StudentName As Name
   Dim StudentAddress As Address
   Dim ID As String
   Dim Grades(2) As Integer
End Structure
```

Although it makes sense to put the definition of the Student structure after the definitions of the structures used to define Student, it is not necessary to do so. The Student structure definition can come before the definitions of Name and Address without causing an error.

Now let's look at a program that uses the Student structure:

```
Sub Main()

  Dim StudentRec(2) As Student
  Dim x As Integer
  For x = 0 to StudentRec.GetUpperBound(0)
    ReDim StudentRec(x).Grades(2)
  Next
  ReDim StudentRec(0).Grades(2)
  StudentRec(0).StudentName.FirstName = "Raymond"
  StudentRec(0).StudentName.MiddleName = "Eugene"
  StudentRec(0).StudentName.LastName = "Williams"
  StudentRec(0).StudentAddress.Street = "123 Oak Park"
  StudentRec(0).StudentAddress.City = "Little Rock"
  StudentRec(0).StudentAddress.State = "AR"
  StudentRec(0).StudentAddress.Zip = "72204"
  StudentRec(0).ID = "03000"
  StudentRec(0).Grades(0) = 83
  StudentRec(0).Grades(1) = 90
  StudentRec(0).Grades(2) = 94
  Dim total As Integer
  Dim average As Single
  For x = 0 to StudentRec(0).Grades.GetUpperBound(0)
    total += StudentRec(0).Grades(x)
  Next
  average = total / StudentRec(0).Grades.Length
  Console.WriteLine("Average: " & average)

End Sub
```

This code demonstrates working with just one student record, but it is easy to see how well it could work with many more records. This example also demonstrates two principles of software design—code reuse and modularity; we'll return to these principles many times in this book. Using the Name and Address structures to build the Student structure makes use of two structures that we can use by themselves or even in other programs that need to keep track of names and addresses. Both Name and Address are sufficiently general that many other structures and/or programs will probably have a use for them.

Defining Student as a composite structure also demonstrates the principle of modularity. By building up the Student structure from other structures, we avoid having to make the definition of Student unnecessarily complex. We can understand what is stored in a student's name by looking at the Name structure definition, which is short and to the point, as is the definition for Address. If we tried to put all those member definitions in one structure, the code becomes harder to read and potentially harder to maintain.

Structure Methods

One of the major difference between structures in VB.NET and structures in other languages (such as C++) is that VB.NET structures can contain methods. A method is the term used in OOP to refer to subroutines and functions. A structure can contain both data members and subprograms that operate on these data.

Let's look at a quick example to illustrate the importance of structure methods. Consider again at the Name structure defined earlier in the chapter:

```
Public Structure Name
   Dim FirstName As String
   Dim MiddleName As String
   Dim LastName As String
End Structure
```

If we want to return the initials from a Name object, we have to write a function to do so:

```
Function GetInitials(aName As Name)
   Return aName.FirstName.Chars(0) & _
    aName.MiddleName.Chars(0) & aName.LastName.Chars(0)
End Function
```

This function works, but we have to put the definition outside the definition of the structure and it isn't intuitive that the function is to be used just with a Name object. A better solution is to enclose the definition of GetInitials in the definition of Name, so that the usage of the function is clear.

A structure definition in VB.NET can include subroutine or function definitions as well as data member definitions. We'll use the term method to cover both types of subprograms. A method definition can be placed anywhere in the structure definition, but it is common practice to put method definitions after the data member declarations.

To add the GetInitials function definition to the Name structure definition, we can just move the definition from outside Sub Main() to inside the definition of Name. The only thing we need to change in the definition is the reference to the aName object, which isn't needed now since we are already inside the structure definition. Here's the code:

```
Public Structure Name
  Dim FirstName As String
  Dim MiddleName As String
  Dim LastName As String

  Function GetInitials() As String
    Return FirstName.Chars(0) & MiddleName.Chars(0) & _
    LastName.Chars(0)
  End Function

End Structure
```

To call the method, we use the dot notation with which we're already familiar from using .NET Framework class objects such as Console.Write, Math.Pow(), etc. Here's how we'd call the GetInitials method using the Name structure:

```
Sub Main()
  Dim myName As Name
  myName.FirstName = "Michael"
  myName.MiddleName = "Mason"
  myName.LastName = "McMillan"
  Dim initials As String
  initials = myName.GetInitials()
  Console.WriteLine("Your initials are: " & initials)
End Sub
```

Now let's look at an example that uses a subroutine instead of a function. One operation we might want the Name structure to perform is to display a person's name in last name, first name format. We could write this as a function and return the name as a string, but just to demonstrate how to do this as a subroutine, we'll assume we don't need to do anything with the value other than display it.

The definition for the LastFirst method is

```
Sub LastFirst()
  Console.WriteLine(LastName & ", " & FirstName & _
                    " " & MiddleName)
End Sub
```

The call to this method looks like this:

```
myName.LastFirst()
```

An important type of structure method you can use in your programming is the *constructor* method. A constructor method is a subroutine that initializes the data members of a structure to a set of values passed to the method when a structure object is declared. Having a constructor method in your structure definition gives you flexibility in how your structure objects are created.

A constructor method is passed one or more values to be assigned to one or more of the data members of the structure. Typically, you will set all the data values in a constructor call, but this is not a requirement.

The following code defines the constructor name for the Name structure:

```
Public Sub New(f As String, m As String, l As String)
  FirstName = f
  MiddleName = m
  LastName = l
End Sub
```

The Name constructor is called in code as follows:

```
Dim myName As New Name("Allison", "Marie", "McMillan")
```

The compiler looks at the combination of the New reserved word with the structure called Name and knows to run the code found in the constructor definition. Structure constructors make working with structures easier since you can assign values to all the data members of the structures in one line of code, rather than having to assign each data member individually after the structure object is declared.

The Constructor Method—New()

New structure objects can be created using a constructor method. A constructor method allows you to declare and assign data to a structure object in one statement, rather than having to use multiple statements for declaration and data assignment. The constructor method handles memory allocation and initialization.

Constructor methods are always named New. The compiler looks for this keyword to begin initializing an object of the structure type. Because constructor methods do not return a value, they are defined as subroutines. Here's a typical constructor method definition, along with the declarations for the data members of the Name structure:

```
Public Structure Name
  Dim FirstName As String
  Dim MiddleName As String
  Dim LastName As String

  Public Sub New(f As String, m As String, l As String)
    FirstName = f
    MiddleName = m
    LastName = l
  End Sub

End Structure
```

The constructor method can be called in two ways. One was is to declare a structure object in one line and call the constructor in another line, like this:

```
Dim myName As Name
myName = New Name("Jennie", "Karen", "Jones")
```

The other way to call a constructor method is to declare the structure object and call the constructor in the same line, like this:

```
Dim myName As New Name("Jennie", "Karen", "Jones")
```

Either method is acceptable, and which method you use will depend on when you need to assign data to the Structure object.

Constructor methods can be overloaded (see Chapter 2 for a definition of method overloading) so that you can have multiple constructor methods. This provides you with more flexibility in how your structure objects can be declared and initialized. For a single structure object to have multiple constructor methods, each method must have a different signature. A method's signature is a combination of the method name and the number and data type of the method's parameters.

We can define more constructors for the Name structure if we so desire. For this particular structure, though, we will define just one extra constructor method that allows just the last name to be set initially. Here's the code:

```
Public Structure Name
   Dim FirstName As String
   Dim MiddleName As String
   Dim LastName As String

   Public Sub New(f As String, m As String, l As String)
     FirstName = f
     MiddleName = m
     LastName = l
   End Sub

   Public Sub New(l As String)
     FirstName = ""
     MiddleName = ""
     LastName = l
   End Sub

End Structure
```

Notice that the new constructor method definition includes assignments for the first name and the middle name. If we left these two assignments out of the definition the compiler would automatically set the two data members to the empty string anyway, but it's considered good programming style to explicitly set data member values to their default values in constructor definitions.

Constructors that contain parameters in their definitions are called *parameterized* constructors. There is another type of constructor, the *default* constructor, that contains no parameters and assigns default values to all the data members. Structures do not allow default constructors, so we will have to postpone their discussion until the next chapter.

A COMPLETE NAME STRUCTURE IMPLEMENTATION

Back at the beginning of the chapter we designed an ADT for a Name object. In this section, we present a complete implement of a Name structure that makes the ADT concrete. Here's the code for the structure and a program to test the structure's methods:

```
Imports System
Module NameStructure

  Public Structure Name
    Dim FirstName As String
    Dim MiddleName As String
    Dim LastName As String

    Sub SetName(f As String, m As String, l As String)
      FirstName = f
      MiddleName = m
      LastName = l
    End Sub

    Sub Clear()
      FirstName = ""
      MiddleName = ""
      LastName = ""
    End Sub

    Sub ShowFirstLast()
      Console.WriteLine(FirstName & " " & MiddleName & _
                        " " & LastName)
    End Sub

    Sub ShowLastFirst()
      Console.WriteLine(LastName & ", " & FirstName & _
                        " " & MiddleName)
    End Sub
```

```
Function ShowInitials() As String
  Return FirstName.Chars(0) & MiddleName.Chars(0) & _
   LastName.Chars(0)
End Function

Sub Copy(ByRef aName As Name)
  aName.FirstName = FirstName
  aName.MiddleName = MiddleName
  aName.LastName = LastName
End Sub

Function Equal(aName As Name) As Boolean
  If (FirstName = aName.FirstName) And _
     (MiddleName = aName.MiddleName) And _
     (LastName = aName.LastName) Then
    Return True
  Else
    Return False
  End If
End Function
End Structure

Sub Main()
  Dim myName As Name
  Dim newName As Name
  myName.SetName("Michael", "Mason", "McMillan")
  myName.ShowFirstLast()
  myName.ShowLastFirst()
  myName.Copy(newName)
  Console.WriteLine("myName copied to newName. _
                  Showing newName:")
  newName.ShowFirstLast()
  If (newName.Equal(myName)) Then
    Console.WriteLine("Names are the same.")
  Else
    Console.WriteLine("Names aren't the same.")
  End If
  newName.Clear()
  Console.WriteLine("Setting newName to new name.")
  newName.SetName("Raymond", "Eugene", "Williams")
  newName.ShowFirstLast()
```

```
      If (newName.Equal(myName)) Then
        Console.WriteLine("Names are the same.")
      Else
        Console.WriteLine("Names aren't the same.")
      End If
   End Sub

End Module
```

The output from the program is

```
Michael Mason McMillan
McMillan, Michael Mason
myName copied to newName. Showing newName:
Michael Mason McMillan
Names are the same.
Setting newName to new name.
Raymond Eugene Williams
Names are not the same.
```

ANOTHER STRUCTURE EXAMPLE—THE RATIONAL OBJECT

We use an ADT to model the data and the operations of a complex data type and we use a structure as a mechanism for implementing the ADT design. In this section we work through the design of a structure for working with rational numbers, from the design of the ADT to the implementation of the Rational structure.

A rational number is a number that can be expressed as a fraction, where the numerator and the denominator of the fraction are both integers. The number 0.75 is rational because it can be expressed as ¾, as is 0.5, which can be expressed as ½. Examples of numbers that are not rational are π and $\sqrt{2}$; neither of these can be expressed as the ratio of two integers.

Computers have trouble working with rational numbers when they are expressed as floating-point numbers, owing to the way floating-point arithmetic is performed in binary. As a result, there can be rounding errors so that an expression that should yield the value 1.0 might actually yield the value 0.999999.

To combat this problem, it can be useful to represent rational numbers strictly as a pair of integers, one for the numerator and one for the denominator. We can design an ADT for a Rational object and then implement the ADT with a structure.

The data we need to store in a Rational object are the numerator and the denominator, both of which are integers. The operations we need include the four arithmetic functions—Add, Subtract, Multiple, Divide—as well as a means of displaying a rational number and a means of comparing two rational numbers to see if they are equal. We also include a method (RSet) for setting the numerator and denominator of a Rational object. We can't use the word Set because it is a reserved word in VB.NET. Using a method such as RSet saves a line of code each time you assign data to a Rational object since in one line you can set both data members. Setting them individually takes two lines of code.

The ADT for our Rational structure is as follows:

ADT **Rational:**
  Data
    Two integers to store the numerator and denominator of a
    fraction.
  Operations
    RSet
      Input: Two integers.
      Preconditions: None.
      Process: Set the numerator to the first integer, set the
                            denominator to the second integer.
      Output: None.
      Postconditions: A Rational object with a numerator and a
                            denominator.
    Add
      Input: A second rational number.
      Preconditions: None.
      Process: Add one rational number to the current rational
                            number.
      Output: A rational number.
      Postconditions: None.
    Subtract
      Input: A second rational number.
      Preconditions: None.
      Process: Subtract one rational number from the current
                            rational number.

Output:	A rational number.
Postconditions:	None.

Multiply

Input:	A second rational number.
Preconditions:	None.
Process:	Multiply one rational number by the current rational number.
Output:	A rational number.
Postconditions:	None.

Divide

Input:	A second rational number.
Preconditions:	None.
Process:	Divide one rational number by the current rational number.
Output:	A rational number.
Postconditions:	None.

Write

Input:	None.
Preconditions:	None.
Process:	Build a string from the numerator and denominator, string separated by a "/".
Output:	A string displaying the rational number as a fraction.
Postconditions:	None.

Equal

Input:	A second rational number.
Preconditions:	None.
Process:	Compare the numerator of two rational numbers and the denominators of two rational numbers.
Output:	True, if the rational numbers are equal; False otherwise.

With the ADT defined, all we have to do is write the code. Here's one definition of a Rational structure:

```
Public Structure Rational

    Dim numer As Integer
    Dim denom As Integer
```

```
Sub Set(n As Integer, d As Integer)
  numer = n
  denom = d
End Sub

Function Add(r As Rational) As Rational
  Dim result As Rational
  Dim tnumer As Integer
  tnumer = numer * r.denom
  r.numer = r.numer * denom
  Result.denom = denom * r.denom
  Result.numer = tnumer + r.numer
  Return result
End Function

Function Subtract(r As Rational)
  Dim result As Rational
  Dim tnumer, tdenom As Integer
  tnumer = numer * r.denom
  r.numer = r.numer * denom
  tdenom = denom * r.denom
  r.denom = tdenom
  result.numer = tnumer - r.numer
  result.denom = tdenom
  Return result
End Function

Function Multiply(r As Rational)
  Dim result As Rational
  result.numer = numer * r.numer
  result.denom = denom * r.denom
  Return result
End Function

Function Divide(r As Rational)
  Dim result As Rational
  result.numer = numer * r.denom
  result.denom = denom * r.numer
  Return result
End Function
```

```
Sub Write()
  Console.WriteLine(numer & "/" & denom)
End Sub

Function Equal(r As Rational) As Boolean
  If (numer = r.numer) And (denom = r.denom) Then
    Return True
  Else
    Return False
  End If
End Function

End Structure
```

The methods of the Rational structure are primarily concerned with performing the correct arithmetic for their particular operation. The algorithms for adding, subtracting, multiplying, and dividing fractions are not complex and can be found in most elementary algebra books (for those of you who have forgotten the specific techniques).

So you can see once more how structure objects are used, let's look at a program that tests the different Rational structure methods.

```
Sub Main()
  Dim r1 As Rational
  Dim r2 As Rational
  Dim r3 As Rational
  r1.Set(2,3)
  r2.Set(1,2)
  Console.Write("Rational number r1: ")
  r1.Write()
  Console.Write("Rational number r2: ")
  r2.Write()
  If (r1.Equal(r2)) Then
    Console.WriteLine("The two rational numbers are _
                    equal.")
  Else
    Console.WriteLine("The two rational numbers are _
                    unequal.")
  End If
```

```
    Console.Write("Let's add the two numbers: ")
    r3 = r1.Add(r2)
    r3.Write()
    Console.Write("Now let's subtract them: ")
    r3 = r1.Subtract(r2)
    r3.Write()
    Console.Write("And now multiplication: ")
    r3 = r1.Multiply(r2)
    r3.Write()
    Console.Write("Finally, division: ")
    r3 = r1.Divide(r2)
    r3.Write()
End Sub
```

The output from this program is

```
Rational number r1: 2/3
Rational number r2: 1/2
The two rational numbers are unequal.
Let's add the two numbers: 7/6
Now let's subtract them: 1/6
And now multiplication: 2/6
Finally, division: 4/3
```

There are several places where we can improve this program in terms of the arithmetic performed. For example, our code for rational arithmetic does not try to simplify fractions once they're computed. It would be easy to add code to do this into the program, but it's not added here so we can focus on the overall process of using a structure as an ADT implementation.

FROM STRUCTURES TO CLASSES

Although structures provide the programmer with powerful techniques for data abstraction and for extending the VB.NET language, they are not the best solution for designing objects to be used in object-oriented programs. Back in Chapter 1, we discussed the three major principles of OOP—encapsulation, inheritance, and polymorphism. Structures only provide us with the ability to perform encapsulation; we cannot perform inheritance or polymorphism with structures. To take advantage of inheritance and polymorphism, we have to use a different type of object for implementing an ADT. This object is the class. A class is much like a structure, in that it lets us define data members and methods for implementing a custom data type with operations. Classes allow programmers to use all three OOP techniques in their code, along with providing other advantages over structures. We begin our introduction to classes in the next chapter and continue studying them throughout the rest of the book.

SUMMARY

The structure is discussed in this chapter as a means of implementing an ADT design. Structures allow us to define the data we want to store in an object, along with the methods (subprograms) that operate on the data. Structures are very powerful objects, allowing us to build a single data type out of, potentially, many different individual data types. The chapter covers basic operations on structures, such as assigning data to structure members, comparing structure objects, and handling structure input and output.

Some operations can be performed on a structure as a whole, such as passing a structure as an argument to a subprogram, whereas other operations, such as comparisons and input/output, must be performed on each member of a structure. Structures can have composite data types as members (like arrays) and you can create arrays of structure objects.

Structures, despite their power and usefulness, are not the final word in implementing ADTs. This is due to the inability of the structure to provide inheritance and polymorphism. These two features of the OOP paradigm are necessary to create a truly object-oriented program. Inheritance and polymorphism, along with encapsulation, are features of class, which is covered in detail throughout the remainder of this book.

EXERCISES

1. Design an ADT for an appointment book. The data in the ADT should include a name, a date, a time, and a comment. The ADT should also include an operation for displaying the data stored.

2. Design an ADT for storing the date. Be sure to include each piece of data that makes up the date, along with the following operations:

   • Display the date in mm/dd/yyyy format.
   • Increment the date by one day.
   • Compare two dates to see if they are the same.

3. Implement the ADT designed in Exercise 1 as a structure. Write a program to test your implementation.
4. Implement the ADT designed in Exercise 2 as a structure. Write a program to test your implementation.
5. Extend the Date structure to include a method for copying one date to another date. Start by modifying your Date ADT, and then write the code to implement the new method.
6. Extend the Appointment Book structure in Exercise 3 by including a method for checking to make sure that two appointments aren't at the same time. Start by modifying the ADT for the appointment book and then write the code to implement the new method.

CHAPTER 4

Classes

This chapter introduces the class, the primary means of implementing OOP in VB.NET. The class framework provides the programmer with many techniques for exploiting the three main principles of OOP—encapsulation, inheritance, and polymorphism.

Classes are somewhat similar to structures in that they allow you to combine data members and methods in the same unit. Classes, though, are much more powerful than structures because they have many more tools available to them. These tools include constructor methods for creating new objects and the capabilities of having multiple methods with the same name and inheriting the definition of one class in another class.

This chapter begins with an overview of class construction, followed by the step-by-step creation of a class, and finally ending with several more examples of creating and using classes. The next few chapters in the book will explore many of the topics we introduce in this chapter.

BUILDING A CLASS

Class construction follows naturally from a well-designed ADT. There are some modifications we'll have to make to our ADT design to incorporate some concepts found in classes but not in structures. Still, a complete ADT makes building a class much easier than if you start from scratch.

The Class Heading

Like a structure, a class definition begins with its heading. The heading of a class consists of an access modifier, the reserved word Class, and a name for the class. To create a class called Name, we would write the following line:

```
Public Class Name
```

Here we are assuming we want the class to have Public access, which means the class can be accessed anywhere in a program that imports the class. There are other access modifiers you can use to define a class, but for now we will just use the Public modifier to keep things simple.

As we discussed in Chapter 2, one of the primary reasons for using OOP is to hide the data of a class from the user of the class. This is part of the principle of encapsulation. When the data of a class are hidden, they cannot be accidentally accessed or changed.

We can explain the concept of data hiding by exploring how data are accessed in a structure. A structure, like the Name structure from the last chapter, has data members for storing data. The data members are declared inside the structure, which provides partial encapsulation of the data. The problem is, each data member can be accessed directly from a program, which violates the principle of encapsulation. Look at the following code fragment:

```
Public Structure Name
   Dim FirstName As String
   Dim MiddleName As String
   Dim LastName As String
End Structure
Sub Main()
   Dim myName As Name
   myName.FirstName = "Michael"
   myName.MiddleName = "Mason"
   myName.LastName = "McMillan"
   . . .
   myName.FirstName = "Steven"
   . . .
End Sub
```

The data members of the structure are directly accessible, meaning that the data members can be changed at will by the programmer. This can lead to problems since the data can be changed in ways not expected by the designer of the structure.

The degree to which we can access a data member in a class is determined by the member's *access modifier*. An access modifier is placed before a variable name in a variable declaration statement in any type of VB.NET program, though we are focusing on data member variable declarations in this chapter. There are several access modifiers in VB.NET, but we will discuss just two in this chapter: Public and Private.

A data member declared as Public can be accessed by any program or any class. This is the most general type of access and should not be used for data members in a class. A data member declared Private, in contrast, can be accessed only by code written inside the class where the data member is declared.

In a class, the data members can be declared as having Private access, which means that the members can be accessed only within the class definition itself, not by the code that uses the class. To begin the implementation of the Name ADT discussed in the previous chapter, we would declare the data members first. Notice that the data member names are prefaced with the letter "p." The "p" indicates that the member is a Private member and also frees up the names to be used with other methods in the class, as you'll see later in this chapter. Here are the definitions of the Name class data members:

```
Public Class Name

   Private pFirstName As String
   Private pMiddleName As String
   Private pLastName As String

   . . .
End Class
```

With our data members declared in this way, we are not allowed to directly access them in the client code. The following line of code generates an error if we try to run it:

```
myName.FirstName = "Steven"
```

The data member is hidden from the view of the client code. We can still provide access to the value in the member, but not directly. We can write a special method, called a Property method, to provide access to set and retrieve the values stored in class data members. We'll discuss these techniques later in the chapter.

Constant Data Members

You can make a data member immutable (unchangeable) by declaring it as a constant. Declaring a data member in this way guarantees that it will not change during the lifetime of the class object.

An example of a constant data member in the Name class is an object that stores a punctuation mark that is used to separate the parts of the name in a display. A value like this is best created as a constant so that if it is used in many places in the class, and the value needs to change, we only need to change it in the class definition. The code for creating the constant is as follows:

```
Public Class Name
    Private fname As String
    Private mname As String
    Private lname As String
    Const PUNCT As String = ","
    . . .
End Class
```

Defined as a constant, the variable PUNCT cannot be changed, either in constructor code or in any other methods defined in the class.

CLASS CONSTRUCTORS

Structures and classes also differ in their use of constructor methods. Classes use these methods to provide the class designer with different ways to declare and instantiate a class object.

There are several different types of constructors you can build into a class. We'll look at two of them in this section—the *default constructor* and the *parameterized constructor*.

Both constructors begin with the reserved word New. A default constructor sets each data member to its default value, according to its type. In other words, an Integer variable is set to 0, a String variable is set to the empty string (""), etc. Default constructors do not have to be defined, but they are as a matter of completeness. If a default constructor is not provided, the compiler automatically sets the data members to their default values.

The following code demonstrates how to define a default constructor for the Name class:

```
Public Sub New()
    FirstName = ""
    MiddleName = ""
    LastName = ""
End Sub
```

In the client code, the default constructor is called when an object is declared like this:

```
Dim myName As New Name()
```

A parameterized constructor allows the client code to pass arguments to the constructor. The constructor method assigns the argument values to the data members of the class. A class will generally have at least one parameterized constructor that sets all of the values of the class data members. This type of constructor is called a fully parameterized constructor.

The following code fragment is the method definition for a fully parameterized constructor:

```
Public Sub New(f As String, m As String, l As String)
    FirstName = f
    MiddleName = m
    LastName = l
End Sub
```

The constructor is called with a line of code like this:

```
Dim yourName As New Name("David", "Allen", "Durr")
```

Alternatively, you can call the constructor after a class object is declared:

```
Dim yourName As Name
yourName = New Name("Raymond", "Eugene", "Williams")
```

As you may have noticed, both the default constructor and the parameterized constructor have the same name. Normally, the compiler complains when you try to name two methods with the same name, but VB.NET allows it because of *method overloading*. Overloading refers to the ability to have more than one method with the same name. However, if you look closely, you'll notice that the methods aren't exactly the same. The default constructor's heading reads

```
Public Sub New()
```

whereas the parameterized constructor's heading reads

```
Public Sub New(f As String, m As String, l As String)
```

The difference is in the parameter list, which along with the name makes up the signature of the method. (See Chapter 3 for a discussion of method signatures.) VB.NET does not allow two methods in a class to have the same signature. Methods that have different parameter lists can have the same name, since they do not share the same signature. Overloading is one of the major features of OOP that make it such a powerful and effective programming environment.

Creating Constructors with Optional Parameters

An alternative to creating multiple constructor methods is to write just one constructor method and use optional parameters to cover the different possibilities when instantiating an object.

Optional parameters are specified in a method's heading by using the keyword Optional, followed by the parameter name and a default value. The default value is used if the parameter isn't specified in the parameter list. The following method computes the sum of up to four arguments passed to it, though only the first two arguments must be specified when the method is called:

```
Function Sum(arg1 As Integer, arg2 As Integer, _
             Optional arg3 As Integer = 0, _
             Arg4 As Integer = 0) As Integer
   Return arg1 + arg2 + arg3 + arg4
End Function
```

The two requirements for optional parameters are that 1. each optional parameter must have a default value and 2. any optional parameters must be placed at the end of the parameter list, after any required parameters.

The DateType class we've been developing in this chapter has three constructors: a default constructor that accepts no arguments; a fully parameterized constructor that accepts three arguments; and a partially parameterized constructor that accepts two arguments, the day and the month, with the year set in the constructor method definition. Here are the constructors again:

```
Public Sub New()
  day = 0
  month = 0
  year = 0
End Sub

Public Sub New(ByVal m As Integer, ByVal d As Integer)
  day = d
  month = m
  year = 0
End Sub

Public Sub New(ByVal m As Integer, ByVal d As Integer, _
               ByVal y As Integer)
  day = d
  month = m
  year = y
End Sub
```

We can whittle these constructors down to just one by writing a constructor method where all the parameters are optional:

```
Public Sub New(Optional ByVal m As Integer = 0, _
               Optional ByVal d As Integer = 0, _
               Optional ByVal y As Integer = 0)
  day = d
  month = m
  year = y
End Sub
```

Creating Constructors with Parameter Arrays

VB.NET provides yet another specialized way to specify the parameters to a method—the parameter array. A parameter array allows you to provide as many arguments to a method as you want, while specifying just the parameter array in the method definition.

A parameter array is specified in a method heading using the ParamArray keyword, followed by an empty array declaration and the data type of the array. The following method heading demonstrates how to use a parameter array:

```
Public Function SumNumbers(ByVal nums() As Integer)_
  As Integer
```

You may notice that the parameter array is passed by value to the method, whereas arrays are normally passed by reference. Parameter arrays must be passed by value since you can't modify the elements in the array. There are a few other rules you must follow when you use parameter arrays:

- A parameter array must be the only optional parameter in the parameter list.
- There can only be one parameter array in the parameter list.
- It must be the last argument in the parameter list.

When you call the method, you have three options for using the parameter array. You can pass an array of the same data type as the parameter array; you can pass nothing, in which case the compiler passes an empty array into the method; or you can pass a list of data values, separated by commas, that represents the data values stored in the parameter array.

Before we discuss using parameter arrays in constructor methods, let's look at a more traditional use of parameter arrays in a function. The following function simply calculates the sum of the arguments passed to it. To make the function as flexible as possible, we use a parameter array in the definition so that any number of values can be passed to the function. Here's the function definition:

```
Function SumNumbers(ByVal ParamArray nums() As Integer)
   Dim x, upper, total As Integer
   upper = nums.GetUpperBound(0)
```

```
  For x = 0 To upper
    total += nums(x)
  Next
  Return total
End Function
```

Here's some code that uses the function:

```
Sub Main()
  Console.Write("The sum of the numbers 1-10 is: ")
  Console.WriteLine(SumNumbers(1,2,3,4,5,6,7,8,9,10))
  Console.Write("Here's another sum: ")
  Console.WriteLine(SumNumbers(10, 20, 30, 40, 50))
  Console.Read()
End Sub
```

Notice that the function call is made first with a list of ten values and the next time with a list of five values. Here's another example where an array is passed to the function instead of a list of numbers:

```
Sub Main()
  Dim x As Integer
  Dim somenums(9) As Integer
  For x = 0 To 9
    somenums(x) = x + 1
  Next
  Console.Write("The sum of the numbers 1-10 is: ")
  Console.WriteLine(SumNumbers(somenums))
  Console.Read()
End Sub
```

Now we're ready to use parameter arrays in our class constructor methods. Using the DateType class again, let's look at one constructor method (using a parameter array) that can replace all the standard constructor methods in the definition:

```
Public Sub New(ByVal ParamArray d() As Integer)
  If (d.length = 0) Then
    day = 0
```

CLASSES

```
        month = 0
        year = 0
      ElseIf (d.Length = 1) Then
        month = d(0)
        day = 1
        year = Now.Year
      ElseIf (d.Length = 2) Then
        month = d(0)
        day = d(1)
        year = Now.Year
      ElseIf (d.Length = 3) Then
        month = d(0)
        day = d(1)
        year = d(2)
      End If
    End Sub
```

The key to using a parameter array in a constructor method is to test the length of the array in the method body. If the length is zero, no arguments were passed to the method and default values are assigned to the data members. If one argument is passed, then the method sets the month data member and assigns default values to the other two members. If two arguments are passed, then the day and the month are set and the year is assigned a default value. Finally, if three arguments are passed, the length of the array is three, and all data member values are set.

Unfortunately, this code is unnecessarily complex. We can write better code using optional parameters for a constructor if we want or need to choose between optional parameters and parameter arrays.

Initializers

Although you will normally use a class constructor to set the values of your class data members, you don't necessarily have to. You can create something called an *initializer*. This sets the value of a data member when an object is instantiated, though not via the constructor.

You create an initializer by setting the value of a class data member when it is declared in the class definition. This value is then used for the data member unless a constructor is called that overrides the value assigned by the initializer. Let's look at an example using the Name class.

In this example we define a DateType class that stores the day, month, and year of a date. The data member for the year is declared using an initializer to automatically set its value to 2003. If a DateType object is instantiated using the constructor that only sets the day or the month, the year for that instance will be 2003. If you want a DateType object to have a different year, there is a constructor method with a parameter for the year that will override the initializer. Here's the code, along with a test program:

```
Module Module1

  Public Class DateType
    Private day As Integer
    Private month As Integer
    Private year As Integer = 2003

    Public Sub New(ByVal m As Integer, _
                   ByVal d As Integer)
      day = d
      month = m
    End Sub

    Public Sub New(ByVal m As Integer, _
                   ByVal d As Integer, _
                   ByVal y As Integer)
      day = d
      month = m
      year = y
    End Sub

    Public Sub Display()
      Console.WriteLine(month & "/" & day & "/" & year)
    End Sub
  End Class

  Sub Main()
    Dim theDate As New DateType(31, 1)
    theDate.Display()
    Dim newDate As New DateType(2, 1, 2002)
    newDate.Display()
    Console.Read()
  End Sub

End Module
```

Property Methods

The second set of methods you define in a class comprises Property methods. Property methods provide controlled access to the data members of your class.

Property method definitions begin with an access modifier that declares the method Public, so that client code will have access to them. Next comes the reserved word Property, followed by the name of the property. The definition heading ends with the reserved word As and the data type of the property. Here is the method heading for the FirstName property of the Name class:

```
Public Property FirstName() As String
```

There are two parts to the body of a Property method—the Get accessor and the Set accessor. These accessors are automatically provided by the compiler when you write the Property method heading. You don't have to define them, but you must implement them in your methods. Let's look first at the Get accessor.

The Get accessor is used to retrieve the value of a class data member. Often the only code in the accessor is a Return statement that specifies a data member name. For example, to return the value of pFirstName, we'd write

```
Get
   Return pFirstName
End Get
```

The Set accessor allows the client code to assign a value to a class data member. The accessor comes with a built-in parameter value that you must use, called value. Although you can write extra code to perform error checking or some other function, a Set accessor is commonly just an assignment statement that assigns the parameter value to a class data member.

Let's look at the Set accessor code for the FirstName Property method, along with the Get accessor:

```
Public Property FirstName() As String
   Get
     Return pFirstName
   End Get
```

```
   Set (ByVal value As String)
     pFirstName = value
   End Set
End Property
```

Property methods are not required in a class definition. You can write your own methods to access class data members, but it seems senseless not to take advantage of the built-in Property methods provided by VB.NET.

Writing Methods for Classes

Methods (functions and subroutines) are used to perform operations on class data members. Methods written for a class are much like the functions and subroutines you've written in procedural code, except that all the data being operated on are, usually, contained inside the class.

Methods in classes are written, as usual, by first writing a method heading. The method heading declares the scope of the method, the type of method being written (subroutine or function), the name of the method, a parameter list, and the return type of the method. The general form of a method declaration is

```
Modifier Subprogram-type Method-name (parameter list)_
  As DataType
```

There are several possible modifiers we can use when declaring a method in a class. For now we will discuss just two, Public and Private. Of these, the modifier we use depends on how we intend to use the method. If we are writing a method that we want the client code to access, we will use the Public modifier. If we are writing a method that is used only inside the class, we declare the method to be Private.

Public methods are much like the methods we wrote when working with structures. A method declared as Public is meant to be accessed by other programs outside the class. For example, a method that displays the full name of a Name object is written as a Public method.

A Private method is usually a helper method used in conjunction with other methods in a class. There is no intent by the class designer to make the method accessible to other programs.

There are other considerations we have to make when writing methods in classes, but you should already be familiar with these issues, such as whether to use a subroutine or a function, what parameters to use, and selecting the return type of the method.

Let's define two methods for the Name class, a Public method Display and a Private method NumChars, that return the total number of characters in the data members of the Name object:

```
Public Sub Display()
   Return FirstName & " " & MiddleName & " " & LastName
End Sub

Private Function NumChars(first As String, _
                          middle As String, _
                          last As String)
   Return first.Length + middle.Length + last.Length
End Function
```

Method Overloading

We've already discussed overloading in conjunction with constructor methods, but we can use overloading with other methods as well. As with constructors, the key to overloading is to make sure each method has a different type signature so that the compiler can distinguish among them.

Method overloading allows us to use a single method in different ways. For example, a class that keeps track of approximate numbers ("around 40") will need to be able to perform arithmetic on both other approximate numbers and "normal" numbers. We don't want to force the user to use different names for the same operation, so we need to overload the arithmetic methods we define for the class.

The following code fragment from a class definition for the ApproxNumber class demonstrates how we can use method overloading:

```
Public Sub Mult(n As Integer)
  Me.data = Me.data * n
  Me.flag = True
End Sub
```

```
Public Sub Mult(app As ApproxNumber)
  Me.data = Me.data * app.data
  Me.flag = True
End Sub
```

Here's another code fragment that demonstrates how to use these methods:

```
Dim num1 As New ApproxNumber(40, True)
Dim num2 As New ApproxNumber(10, True)
Dim n As Integer = 2
num1.Mult(num2)
num2.Mult(n)
```

This overloading technique is based on the type signature of the method. The two methods are said to be *parametrically* overloaded. The first Mult method defined here has an integer as its parameter, whereas the second Mult method has an ApproxNumber object as its parameter. There is no conflict between these two methods because at compile-time the compiler disambiguates the methods by inspecting each method's parameters. This is the same type of overloading used for constructor methods.

Implementing the ToString Method From Object

When a class object is instantiated, it's "value" is a string that identifies the project, the name of the assembly, and the name of the class. For example, if we instantiate an object of the Name class in a project named NameClass inside a Console Application, it is stored as:

```
NameClass.Module1+Name
```

To examine this in more depth, the following program instantiates a set of Name objects, stores them in an array, and then iterates over the array, accessing each Name object in the array:

```
Sub Main()
  Dim names(4) As Name
  Dim n1 As New Name("Raymond", "Eugene", "Williams")
  Dim n2 As New Name("Michael", "Mason", "McMillan")
```

```
Dim n3 As New Name("Bernica", "Mary", "Tackett")
Dim n4 As New Name("Clayton", "Joseph", "Ruff")
Dim n5 As New Name("David", "Dean", "Durr")
names(0) = n1
names(1) = n2
names(2) = n3
names(3) = n4
names(4) = n5
Dim index As Integer
For index = 0 To names.GetUpperBound(0)
   Console.WriteLine(names(index))
Next
Console.Read()
End Sub
```

The output from this program is:

```
NameClass.Module1+Name
NameClass.Module1+Name
NameClass.Module1+Name
NameClass.Module1+Name
NameClass.Module1+Name
```

which is not what we want to see.

When we access a class object in the manner shown above, we want to see values that indicate the current state of the object. We can achieve this goal by creating a ToString method that displays some or all of the values stored in the class object's data members. It is not sufficient, however, just to build the method; we have to override the method because Object (the object that all other objects in VB.NET inherit from) already has an implementation of this method.

Here is a definition of the ToString method for the Name class:

```
Public Overrides Function ToString() As String
   Return first & " " & middle & " " & last
End Function
```

Now when we run the program from above, the full name for each object is displayed.

It is strongly recommended that you implement the ToString method for every class you create. It is unacceptable for the user of a class to accidentally (or purposely) reference an object expecting to see the values representing the state of the object and instead see the internal name of the object.

An Extended Example—The Time Class

In this section we work through an extended class definition for a class that helps us track the time. This class is not necessarily written to replace the DateTime class already found in the language, but it demonstrates the class-building process using a complex data type with which we're all familiar.

An ADT for the Time Class

A class that stores the time must have data members for the hours, minutes, and seconds. Each of these fields will be of Integer type, though we could use Single to track fractional seconds. However, that introduces more complexity than we want to deal with here, so we'll limit our class objects to storing whole numbers only.

The operations we want to perform on a Time object are as follows:

- Constructor to set the default time (00:00:00).
- Property methods to set, modify, and display each part of the time.
- Set the time of an existing Time object.
- Display the time in standard hh:mm:ss format.
- Compare two Time objects for strict equality.

The ADT for the Time class looks like this:

ADT **Time:**
  Data
    Hours, minutes, and seconds as integers.
  Operations
    Constructor
      Set hours, minutes, seconds to 0.
    Property Hours
      Parameter: An Integer variable.

Process: Set hours.
Return: Hours.
Property Minutes
    Parameter: An Integer variable.
    Process: Set minutes.
    Return: Minutes.
Property Seconds
    Parameter: An Integer value.
    Process: Set seconds.
    Return: Seconds.
Display
    Return time in hh:mm:ss format.
Equals
    Parameter: A Time object.
    Process: Compare parameter to current object for equality.
    Return: Boolean value.
TSet
    Parameters: Three integers, for hours, minutes, and seconds.
    Process: Assign parameters to private data members.
    Return: No return value.

Implementing the Time Class

The ADT gives us a blueprint for designing the Time class. We can take the descriptions of each data item and operation and implement them in VB.NET code. In the following sections we'll write the code for the Time class, paying attention to concepts critical to the design of a robust and efficient class.

Declaring the Private Data Members

The Time class needs three data members for the hours, minutes, and seconds. We can declare them as integers, since in the ADT we acknowledged that we won't worry about data such as fractional seconds. Here is the code:

```
Private pHours As Integer
Private pMinutes As Integer
Private pSeconds As Integer
```

We use the Private modifier to hide the data members from the client program that uses the class. If we had made the members Public, they would be easily accessible from anywhere in the client program.

We'll use Property methods to allow the user of the class access to the data members while controlling exactly how the data are accessed.

A Default Constructor Method

All classes should have at least one constructor method—the default constructor—for properly instantiating a new object of the class type. The default constructor is so named because it is used to assign the default data type values to the private data members of the class. The default value for an Integer variable is 0; the default value for a String variable is "" (empty string).

The default constructor is called when you declare a new object of a class type (a process we called instantiation). An example of a new class object declaration is

```
Dim theTime As New Time
```

The reserved word New is used to call the constructor for the class. Here's the code for the default constructor method:

```
Public Sub New()
  pHours = 0
  pMinutes = 0
  pSeconds = 0
End Sub
```

Figure 4.1 illustrates what happens in memory when a default constructor is called.

Using Property Methods

Property methods provide us with a built-in means of writing code to set and return the values of private data members. If you want the user of your class to be able to access the value of a data member and change its value, you should create a Property method for the data member.

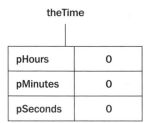

theTime

pHours	0
pMinutes	0
pSeconds	0

FIGURE 4.1. theTime Object Instantiated with Default Constructor

A Property method of this type consists of two parts: 1. a Get accessor for returning the data in a data member and 2. a Set accessor for assigning a value to the data member. The Set accessor has a built-in parameter, value, that will automatically be assigned whatever value is assigned to it in the client code. For example, the following line of code will set the value for pHours:

```
theTime.Hours = 10
```

The Get section works like a function, returning the data stored in the data member when the Property method is called.

```
Console.Write("The hour is: " & theTime.Hours)
```

Here are the complete Property method definitions for the Time class:

```
Public Property Hours() As Integer
  Get
    Return pHours
  End Get
  Set (ByVal value As Integer)
    pHours = value
  End Set
End Property

Public Property Minutes() As Integer
  Get
    Return pMinutes
  End Get
  Set (ByVal value As Integer)
    pMinutes = value
  End Set
End Property
```

```
Public Property Seconds() As Integer
  Get
    Return pSeconds
  End Get
  Set (ByVal value As Integer)
    pSeconds = value
  End Set
End Property
```

Creating a Display Method

The Display method is used to display the time in a Time object. We first need to decide whether to write the method as a function or as a subroutine. Although writing the method as a subroutine is the simplest choice, we gain more flexibility if we write the method as a function.

The method needs to display the time in the standard hh:mm:ss format. Since different parts of the time will be stored as a single digit, our method needs to check the number of digits in the data member and add a leading "0" if the number is a single digit. This is easier to do if the number is in String format, so the first thing we do is convert each data member from Integer to String before checking for the number of digits. Here's the code for the Display method:

```
Public Function Display() As String
  Dim hrs, mns, secs As String
  hrs = CStr(pHours)
  If (hrs.Length < 2) Then
    hrs = "0" & hrs
  End If
  mns = CStr(pMinutes)
  If (mns.Length < 2) Then
    mns = "0" & mns
  End If
  secs = CStr(pSeconds)
  If (secs.Length < 2) Then
    secs = "0" & secs
  End If
  Return hrs & ":" & mns & ":" & secs
End Function
```

Testing Two Time Objects for Equality

Our Time ADT calls for a method that tests two Time objects to see if they're equal. This test involves comparing the individual data members of each object. If pHours, pMinutes, and pSeconds are the same for both objects, then the objects are equal. Otherwise, the two objects are not equal.

Let's look at the code before we explain how it works:

```
Public Function Equal(aTime As Time) As Boolean
  If (Me.pHours = aTime.pHours) And _
     (Me.pMinutes = aTime.pMinutes) And _
     (Me.pSeconds = aTime.pSeconds) Then
    Return True
  Else
    Return False
  End If
End Function
```

The code for the Equal method makes use of the Me reserved word. The Me object refers to the current object in the method definition. Using Me makes your code more understandable and easier to read. Anyone reading your code will know immediately that the data members on the left side of the equal sign are part of the calling object and not some other object. However, we can write the Equal method without using Me if we choose to:

```
Public Function Equal(aTime As Time) As Boolean
  If (pHours = aTime.pHours) And _
     (pMinutes = aTime.pMinutes) And _
     (pSeconds = aTime.pSeconds) Then
    Return True
  Else
    Return False
  End If
End Function
```

Setting the Time of an Existing Time Object

To set the time of an existing Time object, we need a method that assigns values to each of the three private data members. This method is written as a subroutine since we don't need to return a value.

The method will have three parameters, all integers representing the hours, the minutes, and the seconds of the time. The body of the method consists only of assignment statements. Here's the code:

```
Public Sub TSet(h As Integer, m As Integer, _
                s As Integer)
  pHours = h
  pMinutes = m
  pSeconds = s
End Sub
```

Now let's look at a test program that checks the behavior of our class:

```
Sub Main()
  Dim theTime As New Time()
  Dim newTime As New Time()
  Dim sameTime As New Time()
  theTime.Hours = 11
  theTime.Minutes = 27
  theTime.Seconds = 0
  newTime.Hours = 12
  newTime.Minutes = 04
  newTime.Seconds = 0
  sameTime.TSet(11,27,0)
  Console.WriteLine("The old time is: " & _
                    theTime.Display())
  Console.WriteLine("The new time is: " & _
                    newTime.Display())
  If (theTime.Equal(newTime)) Then
    Console.Write("They are equal.")
  Else
    Console.Write("They are not equal.")
  End If
  If (sameTime.Equal(theTime)) Then
    Console.WriteLine("The two times are equal.")
  Else
    Console.WriteLine("The two times are unequal.")
  End If
  newTime.TSet(5,19,0)
```

```
Console.WriteLine("The new reset time is: " & _
                  newTime.Display())
End Sub
```

The output from this program is:

*

```
05:19:00
```

Time Class Additions and Modifications

The definition for the Time class just given is enough to get you started, but there are many things we can do to make the class more powerful and flexible. We'll start by looking at creating static data members.

Shared Data Members

A shared data member is a class variable whose value is retained and can be changed with each instantiation of a class object. Shared data members are most frequently used when you want to keep track of how many instances of a class have been created. We use the Shared reserved word to indicate that the data member doesn't belong to any one instance of the class but belongs to the class as a whole.

When we declare a Shared data member, we also have to use an initializer to assign the variable an initial value. This is because we can't assign the initial value of the data member each time a constructor is called. We want to increment the value of the variable within a constructor call to indicate that a new instance has been created:

```
Private Shared pNumObjs As Integer = 0
```

To keep track of the number of instances of the class created, we include a line of code in each constructor that increments the value of pNumObjs by 1, as in, for example,

```
Public Sub New(h As Integer, m As Integer, s As Integer)
   pHours = h
   pMinutes = m
```

```
    pSeconds = s
    pNumObjs += 1
End Sub
```

Even though a shared data member is part of the class and not any one instance of a class, you cannot access the value of a shared data member from the class object. We'll look at this in more detail in the next section.

Read-Only Property Methods

As you recall, Property methods are used to access and, possibly, change the values of private data members. In many class designs, however, you will want to prevent the client code from changing the value of a data member, while still allowing the client to access its value. You can do this with a read-only Property method.

You make a property read-only by using the reserved word ReadOnly in the property's heading. When you declare a property read-only, you will only write a Get accessor for the property. You can't change the value of the property so you don't need a Set accessor.

To demonstrate how read-only Property methods work, let's create one for the shared data member created previously. Here's the code:

```
Public ReadOnly Property Num() As Integer
  Get
     Return pNumObjs
  End Get
End Property
```

Now, when we want to see how many Time objects we have, we can simply access the Num property, as shown in the following code fragment:

```
Dim theTime As New Time(20,23,0)
Console.WriteLine("Number of objects: " & theTime.Num)
Dim someTime As New Time(5,45,0)
Console.WriteLine("Number of objects: " & someTime.Num)
```

As we already mentioned, we can only access a shared data member's value from an instance of a class. If you try to access it from a class, like this:

```
Console.WriteLine("Number of objects: " & Time.Num)
```

you'll get an error saying you can't reference the data member without an object reference (a instance of the class).

Parameterized Constructors

The default constructor works well when all we want to do is instantiate a class object without adding any data to the object. There are times, though, when we'll want to instantiate an object and store data in some or all of the data members. We can do this with one or more parameterized constructors.

A parameterized constructor consists of passed data, which are then assigned to the data members of the class object. You can have more than one parameterized constructor in a class. In other words, in our Time definition, there will be more than one method named New. This is an example of method overloading. Methods can be overloaded in VB.NET as long as their signatures are different.

A method's signature is the parameter list that accompanies the method name. Let's look at an example of a constructor that assigns data to all the data members:

```
Public Sub New(h As Integer, m As Integer, s As Integer)
   pHours = h
   pMinutes = m
   pSeconds = s
End Sub
```

This method looks similar to the TSet method we defined earlier. It performs the same function, assigning data to the data members of the class object, but it performs this task at the time the object is being instantiated. Here's how we call this constructor method in a client program:

```
Dim theTime As New Time(18,16,0)
```

We now have two constructor methods for the class:

```
Public Sub New()
   pHours = 0
   pMinutes = 0
   pSeconds = 0
End Sub
```

```
Public Sub New(h As Integer, m As Integer, s As Integer)
   pHours = h
   pMinutes = m
   pSeconds = s
End Sub
```

The compiler has no trouble keeping the two methods separate because their signatures are different. The default method has no parameters and the other method has three parameters. Since we haven't yet used all the combinations of parameters that yield different signatures, we can write still more constructors.

One constructor we might want is one that sets just the hour of the time, leaving the minutes and seconds at zero. The code for this constructor is:

```
Public Sub New(h As Integer)
   pHours = h
   pMinutes = 0
   pSeconds = 0
End Sub
```

We can also define a constructor that sets both the hour and the minutes, setting the seconds automatically to 0:

```
Public Sub New(h As Integer, m As Integer)
   pHours = h
   pMinutes = m
   pSeconds = 0
End Sub
```

We have now run out of constructors to write because we've used all the signature combinations. But what about setting just minutes alone and just setting seconds alone? We can't write constructors for either of these scenarios because the signatures would look exactly like the signature for the constructor method that set the hour. Having a different signature means the parameters must differ in number and/or data type.

As an example, look at the possible constructor for setting just the minutes of a Time object:

```
Public Sub New(m As Integer)
   pHours = 0
```

```
    pMinutes = m
    pSeconds = 0
  End Sub
```

The signature for this method looks just like the signature for this method (which sets the hour):

```
  Public Sub New(h As Integer)
    pHours = h
    pMinutes = 0
    pSeconds = 0
  End Sub
```

The compiler cannot distinguish between these two methods because the number of parameters is the same and the data types are the same. The solution to this problem is to use Property methods, as we did earlier in this chapter.

COPY CONSTRUCTORS

A copy constructor allows you to instantiate a new class object by passing the new object another object of the same class. The data members from the existing object are assigned to the data members of the new object, leaving you with two objects with the same data member values.

The code for a copy constructor for the Time class is as follows:

```
  Public Sub New(aTime As Time)
    pHours = aTime.pHours
    pMinutes = aTime.pMinutes
    pSeconds = aTime.pSeconds
  End Sub
```

The copy constructor is invoked when you instantiate a new Time object and pass an existing Time object to the constructor:

```
  Dim theTime As New Time(20,10,0)
  Dim newTime As New Time(theTime)
```

Shared Methods

The properties and methods that make up a class can be either class methods or instance methods. An instance method is associated with an instantiation of a class type, whereas a class method is associated with both the class and the instances of a class. An instance method is used when you want to work with the data associated with a particular instance of an object. For example, if we instantiate a class object, as

```
Dim theTime As New Time(21,30,0)
```

we call the Display method to show the data member values for the object we created.

Now suppose we have a method that can display the current system time stored in the computer. We'd like to have access to that method even if we don't have an instance of a Time object. We can accomplish this by writing the method as a Shared method, which means the method would be available both to the class and to an instance of the class.

A Shared method is like a global method in that you can invoke the method just from the class alone, without having to have an instance of the class. This can be a great advantage if you need to call the method several times, since now you won't have to clutter up your program with class instance names that you don't really need.

A Shared method is created using the Shared reserved word. The following code creates a Shared method CurrentTime that displays the system time:

```
Shared Function CurrentTime() As String
   Dim nw As DateTime = System.DateTime.Now
   Return nw.Hour & ":" & nw.Minute & ":" & nw.Second
End Function
```

The method can then be called directly by referencing the class name and the method name:

```
Console.WriteLine(Time.CurrentTime())
```

You can also call a Shared method from an instance of a class, like this:

```
Dim newTime As New Time(22, 12, 0)
Console.WriteLine(newTime.CurrentTime())
```

An interesting use of shared methods is in a class that can have no instances. An example of such a class in VB.NET is the Math class. The Math class exists solely so we can use the methods of the class for mathematical calculations. You cannot create an instance of the Math class.

An "instanceless" class is created by making the sole constructor method of the class private. Since the constructor can't be called, you can't create an instance of the class, and the only way the class can be used is via any shared methods defined in the class.

In the following example, the class TimeMethods is written with a Private constructor method and a method for displaying the current time and the current date. Although we don't need a class to perform these operations normally, they provide a good illustration of how to create such a class. Here is the code:

```
Module Module1
  Public Class TimeMethods
    Private Sub New()
    End Sub
    Shared Sub ShowTime()
      Dim theTime As DateTime = Now
      Console.WriteLine(theTime.Hour & ":" & _
                        theTime.Minute & _
                        ":" & theTime.Second)
    End Sub
    Shared Sub ShowDate()
      Dim theTime As DateTime = Now
      Console.WriteLine(theTime.Month & "/" & _
                        theTime.Day & _
                        "/" & theTime.Year)
    End Sub
  End Class

  Sub Main()
    Console.WriteLine("The time is: ")
    TimeMethods.ShowTime()
```

```
      Console.WriteLine("The date is: ")
      TimeMethods.ShowDate()
      Console.Read()
   End Sub

End Module
```

Class Object Collections

Grouping class objects into data structures makes it easy to perform operations on all the instantiated objects in a class. For example, suppose we have a group of time objects and we need to adjust their values for daylight saving time. Having all the objects in data structures allows us to just loop through the collection, decrementing each object in turn.

There are two data structures we can consider for grouping class objects—the array and the collection. We discuss the use of these data structures in this section.

Creating Arrays of Class Objects

One way to work with a group of class objects is to store them in an array. Once they're in the array, it's easy to iterate over the array to access each object. You can create an array of a class object type in the same way you create an array of, say, String type:

```
Dim dates(9) As DateType
```

To assign data to the array, you instantiate an array element like this:

```
dates(0) = New DateType(2, 3)
dates(1) = New DateType(2, 4)
dates(2) = New DateType(2, 5)
dates(3) = New DateType(2, 6)
```

Once the data are in the array, we can gain access to the array elements just like we do with any other array type. The following code fragment loops through the array, calling the Display method for each DateType array element:

```
Dim j, upper As Integer
upper = dates.GetUpperBound(0)
For j = 0 To upper
  dates(j).Display()
Next
```

This example demonstrates how to use indexed access to the array, but we can also use a For Each loop for access:

```
Dim aDate As DateType
For Each aDate In dates
  aDate.Display()
Next
```

The For Each loop uses an enumerator to pull each item out of the array. The enumerator is responsible for moving through the array, making sure that the loop doesn't go out of bounds, causing an error.

Storing Class Objects in a Collection

A second data structure you can use for storing class objects is a collection. A collection is a more general data structure than an array and makes adding and accessing data elements easier.

Collections are easier to use than arrays because you don't have to specify an index when adding data or retrieving data from an array (though indexes can be used in collections). We use a collection because we want to have easy access to all the class objects in a program, not because we want fast access (as with arrays) to any one class object in the collection.

There are two strategies we can use for storing class objects in collections. One is to create a collection in the program that uses the class and store all the class objects there. This solution works but is still somewhat inefficient because for each class object we instantiate, we have to add a line of code to add the object to the collection.

A more efficient solution is to create a public collection inside the class and add a new object to the collection at the end of the constructor methods. Here's a sample class definition that follows this strategy:

```
Public Class DateType
  Private day As Integer
  Private month As Integer
  Private year As Integer
  Public dateColl As New Collection()

  Public Sub New(ByVal m As Integer, ByVal d As _
                 Integer, ByVal y As Integer)
    month = m
    day = d
    year = y
    dateColl.Add(Me)
  End Sub

  Public Sub New()
    month = 0
    day = 0
    year = 0
    dateColl.Add(Me)
  End Sub

  Public Sub Display()
    Console.WriteLine(month & "/" & day & "/" & _
                      Now.Year)
  End Sub
End Class
```

The following program uses this class, demonstrating how to pull the objects out of the collection to display the dates stored in them:

```
Sub Main()
  Dim tday As New DateType(2, 6, 2003)
  Dim yday As New DateType(2, 5, 2003)
  Dim d As DateType
  For Each d In yday.dateColl
    d.Display()
  Next
  Console.Read()
End Sub
```

Notice that we define the variable d as DateType, not Object. If we use an Object variable in the For Each loop, then we would have to use the CType function to convert the Object to DateType to view each DateType object's values:

```
Sub Main()
  Dim tday As New DateType(2, 6, 2003)
  Dim yday As New DateType(2, 5, 2003)
  Dim d As Object
  For Each d In yday.dateColl
    CType(d, DateType).Display()
  Next
  Console.Read()
End Sub
```

This is only true if Option Strict is on. If it is off, then we can use an Object variable with the DateType methods and the compiler makes the conversion.

There is an improvement we can make to this program. The way the Date-Type class is defined, we have to call the collection from an instantiated object, which gives the impression that the collection belongs to the instance variable and not to the class. We can remedy this by making the collection a Shared data member. By doing so, we allow the user of the class to access the collection via the class name and not an instance object. The change to the class definition allowing a shared collection is accomplished as follows:

```
Public Shared dateColl As New Collection()
```

The code that uses the collection (along with the class) looks like this:

```
Sub Main()
  Dim tday As New DateType(2, 6, 2003)
  Dim yday As New DateType(2, 5, 2003)
  Dim d As DateType
  For Each d In DateType.dateColl
    d.Display()
  Next
  Console.Read()
End Sub
```

Making the collection a shared data member makes our code easier to understand, since there is now no question as to whether the collection belongs to the class or to an instance of the class.

Yet another way to use collections to store class objects involves creating a strongly typed collection by implementing the ICollection interface and overriding its constructor methods. We discuss this method in Chapter 8.

Nested Classes

A class definition can be nested inside another class definition. You can use a nested class for something simple, such as a defining a novel data type, or you can use one to perform something more essential to the outer class, such as storing outer class objects. In this section we'll only discuss using nested classes as a data type.

An AddressBook class will need to store a name along with an address and a phone number. We've already written a Name class, and it would be a shame to waste all that programming. We could access the class in the normal way, but let's investigate what happens if we define it as a nested class.

A nested class uses the same access modifiers as other classes use. Because we're using the Name class strictly as a data type, and because we won't want access to the class anywhere else, we declare the class as Private. Let's first look at the code for the AddressBook class:

```
Public Class AddressBook

  Private Class Name

    Private fname As String
    Private lname As String

    Public Sub New(ByVal f As String, ByVal l As String)
      fname = f
      lname = l
    End Sub
    Public Property FirstName() As String
      Get
        Return fname
      End Get
    Set(ByVal Value As String)
      fname = Value
    End Set
  End Property
```

```
      Public Property LastName() As String
        Get
          Return lname
        End Get
        Set(ByVal Value As String)
          lname = Value
        End Set
      End Property
    End Class
    Private pName As Name
    Private address As String
    Private city As String
    Public Sub New(ByVal fn As String, ByVal ln As String, _
                  ByVal add As String, ByVal c As String)
      pName = New Name(fn, ln)
      address = add
      city = c
    End Sub
    Public Sub Display()
      Console.WriteLine(pName.FirstName & " " & _
                        pName.LastName  & " " & _
                        Me.address & " " & Me.city)
    End Sub
  End Class
```

The code that uses this class (or classes) is quite straightforward:

```
  Sub main()
    Dim appts As New AddressBook("Mike", "McMillan", _
                                "7200 Walnut", "NLR")
    appts.Display()
    Console.Read()
  End Sub
```

The nested class is called when the constructor for the AddressBook class is called. The Display method uses the property methods of the nested class to pull out the first name and the last name of the Name object instantiated when the AddressBook object is instantiated.

If, for some reason, we want to make the nested class accessible to client code, we have to make the class Public. However, even when we do so, the class is only accessible by qualifying it with the name of the outer class within which it is defined. The following code fragment demonstrates how to use a nested class in this way:

```
Dim aName as New AddressBook.Name("Terri", "McMillan")
Console.WriteLine(aName.FirstName & " " & _
                aName.LastName)
```

CLASS OBJECTS AS OBJECT TYPES

All data types, including classes, inherit from the Object class. A variable declared as Object can take on any data type, meaning that we can assign a class type to an Object variable. However, though an Object variable can be declared and initialized as a class type, you can't necessarily use the variable interchangeably with a class instance.

Although an Object variable can be instantiated with a class constructor, you must explicitly convert the variable to the class's type to access any of the methods. The following code fragment declares an Object variable and then assigns it a DateType value (with Option Strict off):

```
Dim obj As Object
obj = New DateType(2, 8, 2003)
```

To call one of the DateType methods, the CType function must be used to convert obj from Object to DateType:

```
CType(obj, DateType).Display()
```

Even though we have to perform a conversion to get access to the class methods, the Object variable is still considered to be of the class type. You can tell this by accessing the GetType method of the Object variable. The following code fragment creates two Object variables, instantiating one as an object and the other as a DateType instance:

```
Dim obj As New Object()
Console.WriteLine(obj.GetType)
```

```
obj = New DateType(2, 10, 2003)
Console.WriteLine(obj.GetType)
Dim theDate As New DateType(2, 11, 2003)
Console.WriteLine(theDate.GetType)
```

Note that a DateType object is also declared and instantiated so as to compare it with the Object variable instantiated as a DateType. The output from this code is:

```
System.Object
ConsoleApplication12.Module1+DateType
ConsoleApplication12.Module1+DateType
```

These two lines indicate that DateType is defined within the namespace ConsoleApplication12.Module, whereas the Object class is located in the System namespace.

You should not use Object variables in place of class variables (instances), but you can use Object variables to store class data if and when the need arises.

Using Classes in VB.NET Programs

Let us now discuss the practical aspects of using classes with your VB.NET programs. In VB.NET, a class can be defined in the same module as the program that uses the class, or the class can be defined as its own assembly and then compiled into a DLL file so that you can import it into a program. With Visual Studio.NET, you can create a project that includes your main application along with supporting classes, or you can design a class library separate from a program and link it to a program.

Using Classes in Command-Line Programs

In this section we discuss how to separate a class definition from the code that uses the class in VB.NET programs compiled at the command-line. In the next section we'll show you how to do the same thing using Visual Studio.NET.

Classes that exist independently of an executable program are compiled to a dynamic link library (DLL) file. The source code for the class consists only of the class definition. There doesn't need to be a Sub Main since the program won't actually be compiled to an executable. Here's an example of source code that can be compiled as a DLL file:

```
Imports System

Public Class DateType
  Private month As Integer
  Private day As Integer
  Private year As Integer

  Public Sub New(m As Integer, d As Integer, _
                y As Integer)
    month = m
    day = d
    year = y
  End Sub

  Public Sub Display()
    Console.WriteLine(month & "/" & day & "/" & year)
  End Sub

End Class
```

To compile the source code for the DateType class, you issue the following command:

```
vbc DateType.vb /target:library
```

If all goes correctly, a DLL file (DateType.dll) is created.

The next step is to use the DateType class in a VB.NET program. Because we've compiled the class to a DLL file, we can import the class into our program, and then use the class just like we defined it within the program itself. Here's a sample program that uses the DateType class:

```
Imports System
Imports DateType

Module DateTest
  Sub Main()
    Dim theDate As New DateType(3,3,2003)
    theDate.Display()
  End Sub

End Module
```

To properly link the DateType.dll file with our program, we have to add a reference to the command line when we compile the DateTest program. Here's how to do it:

```
vbc DateTest.vb /reference:DateType.dll
```

You can link references to multiple DLL files by separating each DLL file with a comma on the command line, like this:

```
vbc DateTimeTest.vb /reference:DateType.dll,TimeType.dll
```

USING CLASSES WITH VISUAL STUDIO.NET

This section discusses how to build class files using Visual Studio.NET (VS.NET) and then use them in other VB.NET programs. You can build separate DLL files and then import them into a VB.NET program, or you can add a class module to an existing VB.NET program, which allows you to work on the development of both the class and the program at the same time.

Adding a Class File to an Existing Program in VS.NET

One way to build a class using Visual Studio.NET is to add a class file to the existing project. This makes it easier to move from the class definition to the code accessing the class.

Adding a class file to a project is very simple. Select Add Class from the Project window. The Add New Component window appears (Figure 4.2). Select the Class template and name the class (being sure to use a .vb extension). Click Open and a new Editor window appears with a definition template for your new class. The class file is also added to the Solution Explorer window.

You can now work with your class definitions and the code to access them in the same project, which makes development and testing easier. The class files are stored in the same directory as the rest of the project, and only the original source (.vb) files can be seen, so if you want to use these files with other programs, you'll have to compile them separately from the project within which they are defined. One way to do this is to put the code in a class library project and compile it there. We discuss how to do so next.

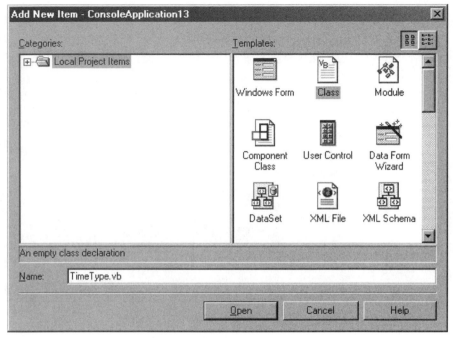

FIGURE 4.2.

Building a Class Library

A class library is an independent project that consists of only a class definition or set of class definitions. A class library can be compiled to a DLL file, which can then be referenced by any other VB.NET program, either command-line compiled or built with VS.NET.

To build a class library, select Class Library from the opening window when you start a new project. You will then go directly to the code editor window, which looks exactly like the editor for a program. The first thing you need to do is rename your file so that the name of the class becomes the name of the file. You also need to access the Property Pages for the file and set the assembly name to the name of the class. However, remove any rootnamespace name to make importing the file easier. A sample Property Pages window is shown in Figure 4.3. Then write the code for your class. Finally, you can compile the class by selecting Build Solution from the Build menu. This creates a DLL file in the subdirectory you selected when you opened the project.

Now you're ready to use the class with a program by starting a new project. Before you can use the class in your program—in fact before you can even

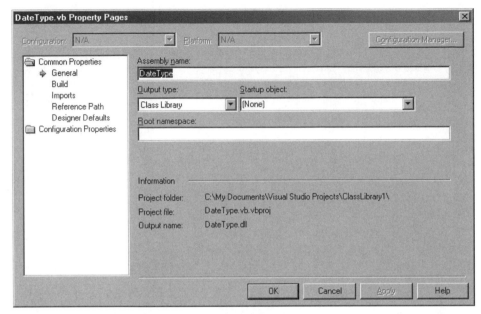

FIGURE 4.3.

import the class into your program—you have to add a reference to the class. This performs the same task we accomplished on the command line by adding the /reference switch to the compile command. You add a reference by putting the mouse cursor over References in the Solutions Explorer window and right-clicking the mouse. You will be prompted to either select a DLL file from a list or browse to find the DLL file you want. For a custom class, you'll have to browse to the subdirectory where your DLL file is stored. Select the file (for example, DateType.dll) and press OK. The file should be added to the references in the Solutions Explorer Window.

At this point you can now import the class and use it in your program. A simple example is the following:

```
Imports DateType

Module Module1
  Sub Main()
    Dim myDate As New DateType(2, 3, 2003)
    myDate.Display()
    Console.Read()
  End Sub

End Module
```

SUMMARY

The class is the primary means for creating custom data types in VB.NET. In this chapter we began our exploration of using classes in VB.NET by discussing how to organize data to be stored in a class object, how to initialize class objects, how to use property methods to allow controlled access to private class data, and how to write methods for modifying class data. We looked at how certain methods and data can be shared among all class objects and we examined the difference between a variable of Object type and a class instance variable. The chapter ended with a practical discussion of how to build classes using both Visual Studio.NET and the command-line compiler that is part of the.NET Framework Software Development Kit.

EXERCISES

1. Design a class that simulates the behavior of a car's odometer. An odometer is an example of a *bounded counter*. As you know, once your car odometer reaches a certain number (which is quite large on digital odometers and 99999 on old analog odometers), the numbers "turn over" and start back at zero. Your class should include a full set of constructors, property methods for setting maximum and minimum values, a method for incrementing the counter, a method for resetting the counter, and a method that returns the current counter value.
2. Write a new method for the Time class discussed in the chapter that displays the time in twelve-hour format, showing times between midnight and noon as "AM" and times between noon and midnight as "PM."
3. Modify the Time class so that the only private data member is seconds. The methods in the class will have to be modified so that hours and minutes are calculated from the seconds of the time.
4. Write Equals, LessThan, and GreaterThan methods for the DateType class discussed in the chapter. Use the behavior of the CompareTo method from the String class as a guide.
5. Create a class that represents estimated integers. An estimated integer is a value such as "around 20." The class should include data members for the integer and an estimation flag indicating whether the value is accurate or an estimate. Write methods for addition, subtraction, multiplication, and division, allowing an operation like 2 + around 20 = around 22.

CHAPTER 5

Access Modifiers

One of the most confusing aspects of OOP is determining the proper access modifier to use for classes and class data members and methods. If you provide too much scope for a data member or method, you risk violating data encapsulation, leading to unwanted data access. If your scope is too restrictive, other classes that need access to a class's data or methods won't be able to access them. In this chapter we discuss the different access modifiers, how they are used to manage class member and method scoping, and when to use each modifier. At the end of the chapter we discuss how these access modifiers work with classes themselves.

The access modifiers available in VB.NET are the following:

- Public
- Private
- Protected
- Friend
- Protected Friend

We also discuss the modifier Shadows in this chapter. A method declared as Shadows in a derived class hides any methods in the base class with the same name. In effect, a method that shadows another method redefines the shadowed method's behavior.

PUBLIC ACCESS

A class member or method marked as Public can be accessed by any part of the class body, by any part of the project in which the class definition is located, or from an assembly built from the project containing the class definition. This is the least restrictive access and is frequently misused by many programmers.

The Public access modifier is usually only used with methods that make up the public interface of the class. If we declare the data members of a class as Public, they can be accessed anywhere in a program. Look at the following class definition:

```
Public Class List

  Public store() As Object
  Public position As Integer
  Public Sub New(ByVal n As Integer)
    ReDim store(n)
    position = 0
  End Sub

  Public Sub Add(ByVal obj As Object)
    store(position) = obj
    position += 1
  End Sub

  Public Sub Display()
    Dim pos As Integer
    For pos = 0 To store.GetUpperBound(0)
      If (Not (store(pos) Is Nothing)) Then
        Console.WriteLine(store(pos))
      End If
    Next
  End Sub

End Class
```

With the data members declared as Public, there is no restriction on what part of the program can access their values. The following program demonstrates what happens when class data members are made public:

```
Sub Main()
  Dim glist As New List(9)
  glist.Add("milk")
  glist.Add("eggs")
  glist.Add("bread")
  glist.Display()
  glist.store(0) = "cookies"
  glist.Display()
  Console.Read()
End Sub
```

The output from this program is

```
milk
eggs
bread
cookies
eggs
bread
```

The line

```
glist.store(0) = "cookies"
```

clearly violates the principle of encapsulation, or data hiding, by allowing the user code direct access to the array that stores the list data. By allowing free access to class data members, we open the class to receiving bad data. One of the main reasons OOP is considered important is the ability of a class to hide its data members from programs that use the class.

When we want user code to access the data stored in class data members, it is best to write Property methods to control how the data members are accessed. Within the Property method, rules can be written that prevent bad or illogical data from being stored within the class object.

As we mentioned earlier, and as you should already be aware the methods of a class that make up the public interface of your class should be declared as Public. If a class method is declared anything other than Public, it may not be accessible from user code. For example, a Private class method can only be accessed inside the class definition. We examine the use of the Private modifier in the next section.

PRIVATE ACCESS

The Private access modifier is the most restrictive of the access modifiers. It is also the modifier you should use most often with class data members. Any member that is declared Private cannot be accessed by any code outside of the containing class definition.

Class data members are declared Private to protect them from outside access. Outside code, whether it's a derived class or user code, cannot directly access a Private variable. Look at the following class definition:

```
Public Class Name

   Private firstValue As String
   Private middleValue As String
   Private lastValue As String

   Public Sub New(ByVal first As String, ByVal middle _
               As String, ByVal last As String)
     firstValue = first
     middleValue = middle
     lastValue = last
   End Sub

   Public Sub Display()
      Console.WriteLine(firstValue + " " + middleValue _
                    + " " + lastValue)
   End Sub

End Class
```

With the data members declared as Private members, we can't directly access them in user code, as we did in the example in the last section:

```
Sub Main()

  Dim myName As New Name("Michael", "Mason", "McMillan")
  myName.Display()
  myName.firstValue = "Steven"  ' This is an error
  myName.Display()

End Sub
```

If we want to provide access to the values stored in the class data members, we need to write Property methods or other methods that can properly set and/or return the values.

Be aware that the default access level for class data members is Private. This means that you can declare data members without any access modifier and they are made Private automatically:

```
Public Class Name
  Dim first As String
  Dim middle As String
  Dim last As String
  . . .
End Class
```

This is considered to be bad programming practice, however, since your data member access intentions may not be clear to everyone reading your code. You should use Private instead of Dim when declaring private data members.

Class methods that are declared as Private are used as "helper" methods inside the class. Derived classes and user code do not have access to these methods. In the following class definition, the function MoveUp is declared Private; its only use is to provide help to the Remove method, which is declared Public:

```
Public Class List

  Private store() As Object
  Private position As Integer
  Public Sub New(ByVal n As Integer)
    ReDim store(n)
    position = 0
  End Sub

  Public Sub Add(ByVal obj As Object)
    store(position) = obj
    position += 1
  End Sub

  Private Sub MoveUp(ByVal n As Integer)
    Dim pos As Integer
```

```
    For pos = n To store.GetUpperBound(0) - 1
      store(pos) = store(pos + 1)
    Next
  End Sub

  Public Sub Remove(ByVal obj As Object)
    Dim found As Integer = Array.IndexOf(store, obj)
    If (found >= 0) Then
      store(found) = Nothing
      MoveUp(found)
    Else
      Console.WriteLine("object not found")
    End If
  End Sub

  Public Sub Display()
    Dim pos As Integer
    For pos = 0 To store.GetUpperBound(0)
      If (Not (store(pos) Is Nothing)) Then
        Console.WriteLine(store(pos))
      End If
    Next
  End Sub

End Class
```

User code cannot access the MoveUp function without generating an error. It is important to understand that data hiding can be useful for more than just the data stored in a class.

PROTECTED ACCESS

Data members and methods declared as Protected can be accessed by their defining class and any classes that inherit from the defining classes, but not from anyplace else. It is common to see beginning object-oriented programmers use Protected access for data members that are part of a class that is inherited later. This makes access to the inherited class's Private data easier, but it also opens a program up to possible problems because of such easy access to data that should be kept private.

Misuse of Protected Access

As a first example of how to use Protected access, let's examine the misuse of Protected with an inherited class. Let's define a Person class, which is then inherited by an Employee class. The data members of the Person class are declared Protected so that we can easily access their values in the Employee class. Here's the code:

```
Public Class Person
  Protected pFirst As String
  Protected pMiddle As String
  Protected pLast As String

  Public Sub New(ByVal first As String, ByVal middle _
                 As String, ByVal last As String)
    pFirst = first
    pMiddle = middle
    pLast = last
  End Sub

  Public Sub New()
    pFirst = ""
    pMiddle = ""
    pLast = ""
  End Sub

  Public Property FirstName() As String
    Get
      Return pFirst
    End Get
    Set(ByVal Value As String)
      pFirst = Value
    End Set
  End Property

  Public Property MiddleName() As String
    Get
      Return pMiddle
    End Get
    Set(ByVal Value As String)
      pMiddle = Value
    End Set
  End Property
```

```
    Public Property LastName() As String
      Get
        Return pLast
      End Get
      Set(ByVal Value As String)
        pLast = Value
      End Set
    End Property

    ' More class code goes here
End Class

Public Class Employee
  Inherits Person

  Private pDepartment As String
  Private pID As String
  Private pSalary As Integer

  Public Sub New(ByVal first As String, ByVal middle _
                 As String, ByVal last As String, _
                 ByVal dept As String, ByVal id As _
                 String, ByVal salary As String)
    MyBase.New(first, middle, last)
    pDepartment = dept
    pID = id
    pSalary = salary
  End Sub

  ' More class code here

End Class
```

How can declaring the data members of the Person class as Protected make writing the Employee class easier? The answer lies in knowing that a Protected data member can be accessed directly. For example, the following code defines a Display method for the Employee class:

```
Public Sub Display()
  Dim name As String = pFirst & " " & pMiddle & " " & _
                       pLast
  Console.WriteLine("Name: " & name)
  Console.WriteLine("Dept: " & pDepartment)
```

```
  Console.WriteLine("ID: " & pID)
  Console.WriteLine("Salary: " & pSalary)
End Sub
```

Notice how the name variable is formed by directly accessing the data members of the Person class. Although this access makes coding easier, it also violates the OOP principle that data member accessibility should be minimized (Bloch 2001, p. 59).

A better method for allowing access to the data in a base class is to declare the data members Private and provide a Protected method in the base class for displaying their values. A method in the inherited class can then call the Protected method from the base class to provide the proper access to the base-class data members.

Using this idea, we can redefine the Person class and the Employee class as follows:

```
Public Class Person

  Private pFirst As String
  Private pMiddle As String
  Private pLast As String

  . . .

  Protected Function showName() As String
    Return pFirst & " " & pMiddle & " " & pLast
  End Function

End Class

Public Class Employee
  Inherits Person

  Private pDepartment As String
  Private pID As String
  Private pSalary As Integer

  . . .

  Public Function Display()
    Console.WriteLine("Name: " & MyBase.showName())
    Console.WriteLine("Dept: " & pDepartment)
```

```
      Console.WriteLine("ID: " & pID)
      Console.WriteLine("Salary: " & pSalary)
   End Function

End Class
```

In summary, you should limit Protected access to base-class member functions and subroutines that need to be accessed by subclasses to gain access to
base-class data member values. Data member access should always be Private
to minimize the accessibility to these values. Of course, there may be times
when you have to violate this rule, but you should do so sparingly and with
extreme caution.

FRIEND ACCESS

A data member or member function (or subroutine) declared with the Friend
modifier can be accessed from any part of the program containing the declaration. Actually, the more proper definition is that something declared Friend
can be accessed only from within the assembly where the declaration is made.
Think of an assembly as a compiled VB.NET program.

   With this in mind, the following program demonstrates how Friend access
works from within an assembly (or program):

```
Module Module1
  Public Class Time
    Friend pHours As Integer
    Friend pMinutes As Integer
    Friend pSeconds As Integer

    Public Sub New(ByVal hours As Integer, _
                   ByVal minutes As Integer, _
                   ByVal seconds As Integer)
      pHours = hours
      pMinutes = minutes
      pSeconds = seconds
    End Sub

    Public Function Display() As String
      Dim h, m, s As String
```

```
    If (pHours < 10) Then
      h = "0" & CStr(pHours)
    Else
      h = CStr(pHours)
    End If
    If (pMinutes < 10) Then
      m = "0" & CStr(pMinutes)
    Else
      m = CStr(pMinutes)
    End If
    If (pSeconds < 10) Then
      s = "0" & CStr(pSeconds)
    Else
      s = CStr(pSeconds)
    End If
    Return pHours & ":" & pMinutes & ":" & pSeconds
  End Function

  Friend Function CurrentTime() As String
    Return (Now.Hour & ":" & Now.Minute & _
          ":" & Now.Second)
  End Function
End Class
Public Class DateTime
  Private pTime As Time
  Private pMonth As Integer
  Private pDay As Integer
  Private pYear As Integer

  Public Sub New(ByVal h As Integer, ByVal min As _
              Integer, ByVal s As Integer, _
              ByVal month As Integer, ByVal day _
              As Integer, ByVal year As Integer)
    pTime.pHours = h
    pTime.pMinutes = min
    pTime.pSeconds = s
    pMonth = month
    pDay = day
    pYear = year

  End Sub
```

```
    End Class

    Sub Main()

      Dim theTime As New Time(10, 30, 0)
      Console.WriteLine("The time is: " & _
                        theTime.Display())
      Console.WriteLine("The SYSTEM time is: " & _
                        eTime.CurrentTime())
      Console.Read()

    End Sub

  End Module
```

The classes Time and DateTime are essentially unrelated except that Date-Time consists of a Time object as one of its data members. Nonetheless, because the data members of Time are declared Friend, the DateTime class can access them directly. Obviously, this is not considered a good programming practice. It cannot be overstated that you should do everything you can to limit the accessibility of class data.

PROTECTED FRIEND ACCESS

The Protected Friend access level is equivalent to the union of Protected and Friend access. In other words, a data member or method declared as Protected Friend is accessible from anywhere in the program in which the declaration occurs, or from any derived class containing the declaration. This is a little-used access modifier and we will not discuss it further.

SHADOWS

Shadowing allows you to define a method in a derived class using the same name as a method defined in a base class, but with different code defining the method's behavior. As with some of the other access modifiers we've discussed, the Shadows modifier should be used with extreme caution, if at all.

Typically, a method is declared as Shadows if the designer of a derived class wants to modify the behavior of a base class method even though the base class method is not overridable. The problem with this is that it's possible the new method will be used in a way the base class designer didn't envision or even explicitly wanted to prohibit. Designers of a shadowing method must test their implementation very carefully to make sure that the method doesn't misbehave in some way.

Let's look at an example of using shadowing. Earlier in this chapter we presented a Person base class and an Employee derived class. The Person class can have a method for displaying a name that is a value-returning function. Here's the code:

```
Public Class Person

  ' Class code goes here

  Public Function Display() As String
    Return pFirst & " " & pMiddle & " " & pLast
  End Function

End Class
```

Notice that this method is not overridable because it is not marked so. The designer of the Employee class wants to use this same name but can't (without shadowing) because the base class method isn't declared with the keyword Overridable. The solution is to shadow the method with another method of the same name, like this:

```
Public Class Employee
  Inherits Person

  ' Class code goes here

    Public Shadows Sub Display()
    Dim name As String = MyBase.Display()
    Console.WriteLine("Name: " & name)
    Console.WriteLine("Department: " & pDepartment)
    Console.WriteLine("ID: " & pID)
    Console.WriteLine("Salary: " & pSalary)
  End Sub

End Class
```

The method defined in the Employee class doesn't resemble the base class method at all. Not only did we change the behavior of the method, we changed the very nature of the method from a function to a subroutine. Yet, because it is declared with Shadows, it can coexist with the base class method. In fact, the shadowing method can even call the method it shadows, as we've shown in this example.

CLASS-LEVEL ACCESS MODIFIERS

Entire classes can be scoped using many of the access modifiers we've been looking at in this chapter. In this section we discuss these modifiers and how you can use them to restrict (or open up) access to your classes. As is this case with data members and methods, the general rule of thumb is to make all classes as inaccessible as possible. We discuss the reasons why in the following.

Class Public Access

Public access is the most common access modifier for classes and one you're surely familiar with by now. A class declared as Public can be accessed by any programs in the current assembly as well as by any linked-in assembly. We won't discuss class Public access any further here since we've been using this access extensively (exclusively) throughout the book.

Class Private Access

We've also already examined Private class access in this book, but only briefly, so we'll take a closer look here.

A class declared with the Private modifier is only accessible within the declaration context in which the class is defined. So what does this mean? The answer depends on the way the class is used, so let's look at several examples.

When a class is declared as Private in a module, it can be accessed by user code and any other class that is declared as Private as well. In the following code sample, the Name class is declared as Private:

```
Module Module1
   Private Class Name
     Private pFirst As String
```

```
    Private pMiddle As String
    Private pLast As String

    Public Sub New(ByVal first As String, ByVal middle _
                As String, ByVal last As String)
      pFirst = first
      pMiddle = middle
      pLast = last
    End Sub

    Public Function Display() As String
      Return pFirst & " " & pMiddle & " " & pLast
    End Function
  End Class

  Sub Main()
    Dim myName As New Name("Michael", "Mason", _
                      "McMillan")
    Console.WriteLine(myName.Display())
    Console.Read()

  End Sub

End Module
```

Clearly, the user can access the class to instantiate Name objects. If we want to utilize the Name class as a base class, the class that inherits it must also be Private. It is illegal to have a derived class with more accessibility than its base class.

A class created as a class library cannot be declared Private. A class can only be declared Private if it is within another type. The Name class defined here was declared Private because its definition was within the scope of the module.

A class is usually declared as Private when it is going to be used as a helper class inside another class. We discussed this scenario in Chapter 4 when we examined the use of a Private class Name in an AddressBook class. As we mentioned in that chapter, a Private class declared inside another class is often called a nested class.

The following program demonstrates again how a nested class can be used within another class to provide help to the containing class:

```
Module Module1
  Public Class Employee

    Private Class Name
      Private pFirst As String
      Private pMiddle As String
      Private pLast As String

      Public Sub New(ByVal first As String, _
                     ByVal middle As String, _
                     ByVal last As String)
        pFirst = first
        pMiddle = middle
        pLast = last
      End Sub

      Public Overrides Function toString() As String
        Return pFirst & " " & pMiddle & " " & pLast
      End Function

    End Class

    Private pName As Name
    Private pID As String
    Private pSalary As Integer

    Public Sub New(ByVal first As String, ByVal middle _
                   As String, ByVal last As String, _
                   ByVal id As String, ByVal salary As _
                   Integer)
      pName = New Name(first, middle, last)
      pID = id
      pSalary = salary
    End Sub

    ReadOnly Property empName() As Object
      Get
        Return pName.toString()
      End Get

    End Property

  End Class
```

```
Sub Main()
  Dim emp1 As New Employee("Michael", "Mason", _
                           "McMillan", "12345", _
                           55000)
  Console.WriteLine(emp1.empName)
  Console.Read()
End Sub

End Module
```

Nesting the Name class inside the Employee class makes the Employee class easier to use, primarily because much of the code for working with the name is encapsulated inside the Name class. Take for example the code for displaying the contents of a Name object (the toString() method). Because this method is found inside the Name class, when we want to display an employee name, we can simply call the toString method of the Name object (pName).

Nesting classes in this manner makes our programs easier to read and use. You can call using nested classes micro-OOP. The advantages of micro-OOP are just as great as they are for us when we use OOP for complete programs.

You may have noticed that the toString method is overridden in the Name class. We had to do this because toString is also a method of the Object class, from which all classes inherit, causing us to have to override toString to use it in our class definition.

Class Friend Access

Friend access is the default access for a class if you don't use any of the other access modifiers. This means that any code within the containing assembly has access to the class. Many of the class examples in this book that are contained in a module could have been declared with Friend access, rather than Public access, but we chose not to do this, however, because we want you to consider your class definitions as available to any program that wants to use them.

To declare a class with Friend access, either use the Friend modifier or just leave off the modifier altogether:

```
Module Module1
  Friend Class Employee
    ' Class code goes here
```

```
    End Class

    Sub Main()
      ' User code goes here
    End Sub
End Module

Module Module1
    Class Employee
      ' Class code goes here
    End Class

    Sub Main()
      ' User code goes here
    End Sub
End Module
```

A class declared with Friend access cannot be accessed by any linked-in program or other classes in a project.

We can use Friend access to our advantage when we nest a class inside a containing class. If the nested class is declared as Friend, we can then access that class through the containing class in user code. For example, in the aforementioned program using the Employee class, we may want to use the Name class to work with names outside of the Employee class. When the class was declared Private, we couldn't use it because it wasn't accessible outside the Employee class.

First, we have to declare the class with Friend access:

```
Public Class Employee
    Friend Class Name
      Private pFirst As String
      Private pMiddle As String
      Private pLast As String

      ' More Name class code here
    End Class

    ' More Employee class code here
End Class
```

Now we can use the Name class in user code:

```
Sub Main()
  Dim emp1 As New Employee("Michael", "Mason", _
                           "McMillan", "12345", _
                           55000)
  Console.WriteLine(emp1.empName)
  Dim spouse As New Employee.Name("Terri", "Lea", _
                                  "McMillan")
  Console.WriteLine(spouse.toString())
  Console.Read()
End Sub
```

Declaring a nested class as Friend gives us the opportunity to use the class outside its container class, even though we have to qualify the name of the class using the containing class name.

Class Shadows Access

Shadowing classes is not a commonly used technique, but it is possible. An example where you might want to shadow a class is if you have a nested class and the containing class is inherited by another class, which wants to have its own nested class with the same name as the nested class in the base (containing) class.

Here's an example using a Person class, an Employee class, and the Name class. The Employee class inherits the Person class, which uses the Name class as a nested class for working with names. The Employee class also wants a nested Name class to make its names easier to work with. Because the Name class in Person is nested, it is not available to the Employee class.

Here's the code for shadowing a nested class:

```
Public Class Person
  Friend Class Name
    Private pFirst As String
    Private pMiddle As String
    Private pLast As String

    Public Sub New(ByVal first As String, ByVal middle _
                   As String, ByVal last As String)
      pFirst = first
      pMiddle = middle
```

```
      pLast = last
    End Sub

    Public Shadows Function toString() As String
      Return pFirst & " " & pMiddle & " " & pLast
    End Function
  End Class
  Private pAge As Integer
  Private pSex As String

  ' More class code here

End Class

Public Class Employee
  Inherits Person

  Friend Shadows Class Name
    Private pFirst As String
    Private pMiddle As String
    Private pLast As String

    Public Sub New(ByVal first As String, ByVal middle _
                As String, ByVal last As String)
      pFirst = first
      pMiddle = middle
      pLast = last
    End Sub

    Public Shadows Function toString() As String
      Return pFirst & " " & pMiddle & " " & pLast
    End Function
  End Class
  Private pID As String
  Private pDept As String
  Private pSalary As Integer

  ' More class code here

End Class
```

Shadowing classes will make your code harder to read and harder to understand. Understandably, you should only use this technique when no other way to solve that particular problem exists.

SUMMARY

Access modifiers define the scope of your data members, methods, and classes. Understanding how they work and when to use them is crucial to a complete understanding of OOP using VB.NET.

Many beginning programmers, especially those new to OOP techniques, tend to make all their data members Public, finding this the easiest way to achieve access to class data members in client code. Such practice is always a bad idea because making class data members Public violates the principle of encapsulation. The preferred technique is to make most class data members Private and create Property methods or accessor methods that provide access to class data member values.

Another common mistake of beginning object-oriented programmers is to make base-class data members Protected because they want those values available to a derived class. This also generally violates encapsulation (though not always) and should be used with care. The best solution, again, for accessing Private data members is to provide Public methods that derived classes can access.

EXERCISES

1. The Rational class defines the data and methods involved in working with fractional numbers. The beginnings of a definition for a Rational class look like this:

```
Public Class Rational
  Private numer As Integer
  Private denom As Integer

  Public Sub New(numer As Integer, denom As Integer)
    Me.numer = numer
    Me.denom = denom
  End Sub

  ' More class code here
End Class
```

Design a nested class (RationalDraw) that displays a rational number in the form—numerator/denominator (i.e., 2 /3, 1 /2, 13/15).

2. Using the bounded counter class developed in a previous chapter, design a derived class, LapCounter, that simulates a hand-held lap counter. The base class should have a method such as Display that displays the value of the counter object. Shadow that method with another method in the derived class that shows both miles and laps completed.

3. Modify the nested class in Exercise 1 so that it is a Friend class to its containing class. Use it to display a Rational object created in your program.

4. Create a TimeType class (or use one you've created before) that includes only Private methods. Include in your class definition methods for displaying the time and for comparing two TimeType objects. Derive a DateTime class from the TimeType class. Modify the methods in TimeType so they can be accessed directly in the DateTime class.

5. Modify the TimeType class built in Exercise 4 so that it has a nested class that stores instances of the TimeType class. The nested class should have a toString method to display all the class instances stored. You may use either an array or an ArrayList to store objects.

CHAPTER 6

Abstract Classes and Interfaces

ABSTRACT CLASSES

As you write more and more complex programs, you will find situations where you want to define classes that are so abstract that you will not want users to implement them directly. Instead, you will want to derive classes from these *abstract* classes that define more specific data and behavior. Abstract classes are implemented in VB.NET using the MustInherit keyword.

A simple example that beautifully illustrates the concept of abstract classes is food. When you go to a restaurant, you don't order just food. You order some type of food, such as steak, or a salad, or apple pie. Each of these is a specific instance of food, sharing some characteristics with the others, while obviously also differing from the others in substantial ways. Abstract classes let us define a high-level abstract object, such as food, that we can then use as a base class for many different derived classes. Because we would never want to instantiate the abstract class, we mark it abstract (MustInherit) so that it is clear the class is to be used as a base class only.

Creating Abstract Classes

To designate a class as an abstract class in VB.NET, we use the MustInherit keyword. Once a class is defined this way, we can only use the class as a base class for other derived classes.

Within an abstract class, we can declare the usual private data members, constructor methods, property methods, and so on. We can define specific behaviors by writing a complete method definition, such as providing specific constructor methods that derived classes can call. We can also create abstract methods, again using the keyword MustInherit, that do not have a definition in the base class. Instead, the method definition is specified in each derived class inheriting from the abstract class.

To demonstrate how we can use abstract classes, let's revisit the Counter class exercise from Chapter 4. In that exercise, you were to build a class that behaved like a car's odometer or a digital clock. This class has a minimum value and a maximum value, as well as a current value. The class has two methods: Increment, for advancing the counter, and Display, for displaying it. Here's the code we use to define the Counter class as a Public class:

```
Public Class Counter

  Private pMin As Integer
  Private pMax As Integer
  Private pValue As Integer

  Public Sub New(ByVal theMin As Integer, _
                 ByVal theMax As Integer)
    pMin = theMin
    pMax = theMax
    pValue = pMin
  End Sub
  Public Sub Increment()
    pValue += 1
    If (pValue > pMax) Then
      pValue = pMin
    End If
```

```
End Sub

Public Sub Display()
  Console.WriteLine(pValue)
End Sub

End Class
```

To instantiate a Counter object, we have to call the constructor method with arguments for the minimum and maximum values:

```
Dim odometer As New Counter(0, 99999)
```

Since every Counter object we instantiate is going to be a particular type of counter, it makes sense to redefine the Counter class as an abstract class, so that we have to derive a specific type of counter every time we want to use the class. We can make the Counter class an abstract class simply by changing the class's heading:

```
MustInherit Class Counter
. . .
End Class
```

Now we have to create a derived class to have a Counter-like object. The following code shows the definition for an Odometer class that inherits from the Counter class:

```
Public Class Odometer
  Inherits Counter
  Public Sub New()
    MyBase.New(0, 99999)
  End Sub

End Class
```

You're probably thinking that this is just a partial definition of the class—but no; this is the complete definition. Most of the behavior is defined in the abstract class, and all you have to do is make a call to the base class constructor with the minimum and maximum values.

Creating a derived class from an abstract class changes how we use the class in a program. When the Counter class was just a class, we had to pass the minimum and maximum values to the constructor method when we instantiated a new Counter object. Deriving a class from an abstract Counter class, however, allows us to instantiate a new class object without having to specify these values. We can embed the minimum and maximum values in the call to the base class constructor, as shown in the constructor method for the Odometer class. This allows the user to instantiate an Odometer object without having to specify the maximum and minimum values, which is in line with the concepts of data hiding:

```
Dim myCar As New Odometer()
```

Using abstract classes differs little from using inheritance. We still need to make a call to the base class's constructor method to initialize the Private data members contained in the base class. If we don't need to change the behavior of the base class methods, we can use them as is. However, if we do want to change the behavior of any of the base class methods, we must redefine the base class methods with the Overridable keyword, just as we do with inheritance. In the following example, we derive the class LapCounter from the Counter abstract class. First, here's the rewritten code for the Counter abstract class:

```
MustInherit Class Counter
   Private pMin As Integer
   Private pMax As Integer
   Private pValue As Integer
   Public Sub New(ByVal theMin As Integer, _
               ByVal theMax As Integer)
     pMin = theMin
     pMax = theMax
     pValue = pMin
   End Sub
   Public Overridable Sub Increment()
     pValue += 1
     If (pValue > pMax) Then
       pValue = pMin
     End If
   End Sub
```

```
    Public Function getValue() As Integer
      Return pValue
    End Function
    Public Sub setValue(ByVal n As Integer)
      pValue = n
    End Sub
    Public Overridable Sub Display()
      Console.WriteLine(pValue)
    End Sub
  End Class
```

We had to make the Increment and Display methods Overridable so we can change their definitions in the derived class. We also added two methods (getValue and setValue) so that we can access the Private data member pValue in the derived class. Of course, we could have made pValue Protected, but then we run the risk of violating encapsulation, so we keep the data members Private and write setter and getter methods for the data member.

The LapCounter class redefines the Increment method and the Display method to reflect the proper behavior of a lap counter. Here's the code:

```
  Public Class LapCounter
    Inherits Counter

    Private miles As Integer = 0
    Public Sub New()
      MyBase.New(0, 3)
    End Sub
    Public Overrides Sub Increment()
      MyBase.setValue(MyBase.getValue + 1)
      If (MyBase.getValue() > 3) Then
        miles += 1
        MyBase.setValue(0)
      End If
    End Sub
    Public Overrides Sub Display()
      Console.WriteLine("Miles: " & miles & " Laps: " & _
                        MyBase.getValue)
    End Sub
  End Class
```

The following code tests the LapCounter class:

```
Sub Main()
  Dim myLaps As New LapCounter()
  Dim x As Integer
  For x = 1 To 15
    myLaps.Increment()
    myLaps.Display()
  Next
  Console.Read()
End Sub
```

Creating Abstract Classes with Abstract Methods

Some abstract classes are so abstract that no specific behaviors can be defined in the class. Some abstract classes will define some class behaviors and leave other definitions to the derived class or classes. If we want to specify methods that must be implemented in the derived class we use MustOverride methods.

A MustOverride method is just a method heading with no body. Any method marked MustOverride must be implemented by a derived class. The functionality of the base class that must be implemented in the derived class is marked as MustOverride in the abstract class. Let's look at a familiar example to illustrate how to use MustOverride methods.

The List class can really be considered an abstract class because there is always some specific implementation of a list that we will want to work with— a list that stores data sequentially, a list that stores data in sorted order, a list that stores data as a set, and so on. We know in advance that all classes derived from the List class will have at least the following methods: Add, Remove, and Display. A SetList class will include other methods (Union and Intersection, for example) that distinguish a set-type list. These methods can be implemented in the derived class and do not even have to be mentioned in the abstract class.

The following code defines an abstract List class:

```
MustInherit Class List

  Protected store() As Object
  Protected position As Integer
```

```
  Public Sub New(ByVal n As Integer)
    ReDim store(n)
    position = 0
  End Sub

  MustOverride Sub Add(ByVal obj As Object)
  MustOverride Sub Remove(ByVal obj As Object)
  MustOverride Sub Display()

End Class
```

Now let's look at a derived class that uses this abstract class as its base:

```
Public Class SeqList
  Inherits List

  Public Sub New(ByVal n As Integer)
    MyBase.New(n)
  End Sub
  Public Overrides Sub Add(ByVal obj As Object)
    store(position) = obj
    position += 1
  End Sub

  Public Overrides Sub Remove(ByVal obj As Object)
    Dim pos, lower As Integer
    pos = Array.IndexOf(store, obj)
    For lower = pos To store.GetUpperBound(0) - 1
      store(lower) = store(lower + 1)
    Next
    store(lower) = Nothing
  End Sub

  Public Overrides Sub Display()
    Dim pos As Integer
    For pos = 0 To store.GetUpperBound(0)
      If (Not (store(pos) Is Nothing)) Then
        Console.WriteLine(store(pos))
      End If
    Next
  End Sub

End Class
```

The important point to remember about abstract classes is that by making the class abstract, and making the methods abstract as well, you allow the derived class to provide a specific definition of its behavior. This definition can be clearer since you don't have to redefine or modify a behavior defined in the base class. This also makes long-term maintenance easier to perform because there is no (or little) code defined in the base class that might be broken if and when the code in the derived class is changed.

Using Interfaces

An interface is a contract that dictates the behavior of a class. When you define an interface, you specify which methods and properties a class using the interface must implement in its definition. The interface does not specify which data members to declare or what the method definitions should look like. An interface is just a list of methods and properties that any class implementing the interface must include in its definition.

Interfaces Versus Inheritance

Choosing between using interfaces and using inheritance is sometimes confusing to the beginning object-oriented programmer. Many OOP novices are more likely to choose inheritance, thinking that deriving classes from a base class is the proper technique to build an object hierarchy. Most times, however, an interface-based design is the proper solution. In this section we'll discuss the whys and whens of using interfaces instead of inheritance.

Inheritance, as we've seen, is to be used when we want to define an *is-a* relationship. For example, car is-a type of road vehicle, as is a truck and an SUV. We might define a road vehicle class like this:

```
Public Class RoadVehicle
  Protected pWheels As Integer
  Protected pDoors As Integer
  Protected pPassengers As Integer

  Public Property Wheels() As Integer
    Get
      Return pWheels
    End Get
    Set (ByVal value As Integer)
      pWheels = value
    End Set
```

```
    End Property

    Public Property Doors() As Integer
      Get
        Return pDoors
      End Get
      Set (ByVal value As Integer)
        pDoors = value
      End Set
    End Property

    Public Property Passengers() As Integer
      Get
        Return pPassengers
      End Get
      Set (ByVal value As Integer)
        pPassengers = value
      End Set
    End Property
  End Class
```

We can then define an SUV to be a derived class of the RoadVehicle base class:

```
Public Class SUV
  Inherits RoadVehicle
  Public Sub New(w As Integer, d As Integer, _
                 p As Integer)
    MyBase.New(w, d, p)
  End Sub
End Class
```

An interface, in contrast, is used to describe a *has-a* relationship. For instance, we can create a BankAccount interface that includes methods for calculating interest and deducting fees. These methods are not actually defined until we implement the interface with an actual class. A PersonalAccount class, for example, will have one method for calculating fees and interest, whereas a BusinessAccount class will have entirely different methods for calculating fees and interest.

When we are modeling a relationship where the lower level objects might differ quite a bit in which methods and properties are implementing, we should use inheritance. When the lower level objects will all have mostly the same methods, yet the implementations of those methods will differ in some way, we should use interfaces.

Creating an Interface

An interface starts with the keyword Interface followed by the interface name. An interface name, by convention, starts with a capital "I" to indicate the entity is an interface. For example, an interface that specifies the methods for a Time class will start its definition like this:

```
Interface ITime
```

The body of an interface consists of function and subroutine (method) headings, as well as Property method headings. The body of an interface cannot contain any data member declarations or the body of any method definition. The interface can specify what data the class is supposed to store by specifying Property methods that are used to assign data to and retrieve data from the implemented class's data members.

The beginning of an interface for the Time class discussed in Chapter 3 would look like this:

```
Interface ITime
   Property Hours() As Integer
   Property Minutes() As Integer
   Property Seconds() As Integer

   Sub SetTime(h As Integer, m As Integer, s As Integer)
   Sub Display()
   Function Equal(aTime As Time) As Boolean
End Interface
```

If you are familiar with the C++ language, you will notice that the code inside the interface looks a lot like function prototypes, which, in essence, they are. When a class is implemented with this interface, the compiler will check to see if each of these methods is included in the class definition and if that inclusion is done using the same heading specified in the interface.

Implementing an Interface with a Class

An interface by itself cannot be used for anything. We have to implement the interface with a class. The class, once it indicates to the compiler that it is implementing an interface, will be required to have a definition for each method listed in the interface.

The first step in creating an interface-implementing class is to indicate that the class is implementing an interface. This is accomplished by placing the reserved word Implements on the line after the class heading, along with the name of the interface, as in, for example,

```
Public Class Time
   Implements Itime
```

The contract between the interface and the class is now in effect. For the class to compile and run, it must implement each of the methods specified in the interface.

A class method that implements an interface method must indicate which method it is implementing. You do this by again using the Implements keyword along with the interface name and the method name. This does not apply to constructor methods, of course, since constructors aren't specified in the interface. Let's look at one of the methods in the Time class that implements a method from the ITime interface:

```
Public Sub Display() Implements ITime.Display
   Console.WriteLine(pHours & ":" & pMinutes & ":" & _
                     pSeconds)
End Sub
```

The reserved word Implements must be on the same line as the method heading. If there's not enough room, use the line continuation character to extend the line to the next line.

An Extended Interface Implementation Example

In this section we present a complete program that demonstrates how to implement an interface. The interface creates a set of methods for building a class for keeping track of dates. We'll show you the code first and then discuss both the interface and its implementation. First, here's the code:

```
Imports System
Module Interfaces

    Interface IDate
    Property Month() As Integer
    Property Day() As Integer
    Property Year() As Integer

    Sub SetDate(m As Integer, d As Integer, _
                y As Integer)
    Sub Display()
    Sub Increment()

  End Interface

  Public Class DateType
      Implements IDate

    Protected pMonth As Integer
    Protected pDay As Integer
    Protected pYear As Integer

    Public Sub New()
      pMonth = 0
      pDay = 0
      pYear = 0
    End Sub

    Public Sub New(m As Integer, d As Integer, _
                y As Integer)
      pMonth = m
      pDay = d
      pYear = y
    End Sub

    Public Property Month() As Integer Implements _
     IDate.Month
      Get
        Return pMonth
      End Get
      Set (ByVal value As Integer)
        pMonth = value
      End Set
    End Property
```

```vb
Public Property Day() As Integer Implements _
 IDate.Day
  Get
    Return pDay
  End Get
  Set (ByVal value As Integer)
    pDay = value
  End Set
End Property

Public Property Year() As Integer Implements _
 IDate.Year
  Get
    Return pYear
  End Get
  Set (ByVal value As Integer)
    pYear = value
  End Set
End Property

Public Sub SetDate(m As Integer, d As Integer, _
                   y As Integer) Implements _
                   IDate.SetDate
  pMonth = m
  pDay = d
  pYear = y
End Sub

Public Sub Display() Implements IDate.Display
  Dim mon, day, yr As String
  mon = CStr(pMonth)
  day = CStr(pDay)
  yr = CStr(pYear)
  If (mon.Length < 2) Then
    mon = "0" & mon
  End If
  If (day.Length < 2) Then
    day = "0" & day
  End If
  Console.WriteLine(mon & "/" & day & "/" & yr)
End Sub
```

```
   Public Sub Increment() Implements IDate.Increment
     pDay += 1
     If (pDay > 31) Then
       pDay = 1
       pMonth += 1
     End If
   End Sub

 End Class

 Sub Main()
   Dim theDate As New DateType
   theDate.SetDate(12,1,2002)
   theDate.Display()
   theDate.Increment()
   theDate.Display()
   theDate.Month = 11
   theDate.Day = 24
   theDate.Display()
 End Sub

End Module
```

The output from this program is

```
12/01/2002
12/02/2002
11/24/2002
```

The implementation of the interface in this example is straightforward. Again, we have to make sure that each method in the class definition specifies which interface method it is implementing. There are several methods in the class that can be improved upon in some way. For example, there should be error checking to make sure that the user doesn't try to enter a day or month number outside the range of proper days and months. There also needs to be a more accurate way to handle the situation where an increment of the Day member moves the month to a new month. These and other improvements to the class are addressed in the exercises.

Implementing More Than One Interface
There's no reason why you have to limit yourself to just one interface when building a class. You can implement multiple interfaces inside one class if

your design calls for it. Let's look at an example that illustrates how this works.

We have previously implemented interfaces for keeping track of the date (IDate) and keeping track of the time (ITime). If we want to build a class that can keep track of both the date and the time, we can implement both interfaces in a DateTime class.

To implement more than one interface, list them repeatedly after the Implements reserved word. To implement both ITime and IDate in the DateTime class, the class heading looks like this:

```
Public Class DateTime
    Implements ITime, IDate
```

The DateTime class, then, will have to implement all the methods defined in both the ITime interface and the IDate interface. Here's the code for both the interfaces and the class:

```
Imports System
Module Interfaces

    Interface ITime

        Property Hours() As Integer
        Property Minutes() As Integer
        Property Seconds() As Integer

        Sub SetTime(h As Integer, m As Integer, _
                 s As Integer)
        Sub TimeDisplay()
        Function Equal(aTime As DateTime) As Boolean
        Sub TimeIncrement()

    End Interface

    Interface IDate
        Property Month() As Integer
        Property Day() As Integer
        Property Year() As Integer

        Sub SetDate(m As Integer, d As Integer, _
                 y As Integer)
        Sub DateDisplay()
        Sub DateIncrement()
    End Interface
```

```
Public Class DateTime
      Implements ITime, IDate

  Private pHours As Integer
  Private pMinutes As Integer
  Private pSeconds As Integer
  Protected pMonth As Integer
  Protected pDay As Integer
  Protected pYear As Integer

  Public Sub New()
    pHours = 0
    pMinutes = 0
    pSeconds = 0
    pMonth = 0
    pDay = 0
    pYear = 0
  End Sub

  Public Sub New(h As Integer, m As Integer, _
                 s As Integer, mo As Integer, _
                 d As Integer, y As Integer)
    pHours = h
    pMinutes = m
    pSeconds = s
    pMonth = mo
    pDay = d
    pYear = y
  End Sub

  Public Property Hours() As Integer Implements _
   ITime.Hours
    Get
      Return pHours
    End Get
    Set (ByVal value As Integer)
      pHours = value
    End Set
  End Property

  Public Property Minutes() As Integer Implements _
   ITime.Minutes
```

```
    Get
      Return pMinutes
    End Get
    Set (ByVal value As Integer)
      pMinutes = value
    End Set
End Property

Public Property Seconds() As Integer Implements _
  ITime.Seconds
    Get
      Return pSeconds
    End Get
    Set (ByVal value As Integer)
      pSeconds = value
    End Set
End Property

Public Property Month() As Integer Implements _
  IDate.Month
    Get
      Return pMonth
    End Get
    Set (ByVal value As Integer)
      pMonth = value
    End Set
End Property

Public Property Day() As Integer Implements _
  IDate.Day
    Get
      Return pDay
    End Get
    Set (ByVal value As Integer)
      pDay = value
    End Set
End Property

Public Property Year() As Integer Implements _
  IDate.Year
    Get
```

```
      Return pYear
    End Get
    Set (ByVal value As Integer)
      pYear = value
    End Set
End Property

Public Sub SetTime(h As Integer, m As Integer, _
                   s As Integer) Implements _
                   ITime.SetTime
    pHours = h
    pMinutes = m
    pSeconds = s
End Sub

Public Sub SetDate(m As Integer, d As Integer, _
                   y As Integer) Implements _
                   IDate.SetDate
    pMonth = m
    pDay = d
    pYear = y
End Sub

Public Sub TimeDisplay() Implements _
  ITime.TimeDisplay
    Dim hours, minutes, seconds As String
    hours = CStr(pHours)
    minutes = CStr(pMinutes)
    If (minutes.Length < 2) Then
      minutes = "0" & minutes
    End If
    seconds = CStr(pSeconds)
    If (seconds.Length < 2) Then
      seconds = "0" & seconds
    End If
    Console.WriteLine(hours & ":" & minutes & _
                      ":" & seconds)
End Sub

Public Function Equal(aTime As DateTime) As _
  Boolean Implements ITime.Equal
```

```
      If (pHours = aTime.pHours) And _
        (pMinutes = aTime.pMinutes) And _
        (pSeconds = aTime.pSeconds) Then
       Return True
     Else
       Return False
     End If
   End Function

   Public Sub DateDisplay() Implements _
    IDate.DateDisplay
     Console.WriteLine(pMonth & "/" & pDay & "/" & _
                       pYear)
   End Sub

   Public Sub DateIncrement() Implements _
    IDate.DateIncrement
     pMonth += 1
   End Sub

   Public Sub TimeIncrement() Implements _ .
    ITime.TimeIncrement
     pDay += 1
   End Sub

 End Class

 Sub Main()
   Dim dTime as New DateTime
   dTime.SetTime(6,0,0)
   dTime.SetDate(11,25,2002)
   dTime.TimeDisplay()
   dTime.DateDisplay()
 End Sub
End Module
```

This example demonstrates how more than one interface can be used to develop a more complex has-a relationship. A DateTime object needs to store the day, the month, and the year, as well as the hours, minutes, and seconds of the current time. If a DateTime object only needed to store part of these fields, than we could have designed the DateTime class as a derived class from a Date class and a Time class.

Implementing the DateTime class using interfaces would be even more important if a DateTime object also consisted of fields that aren't part of either the Date class or the Time class. A general rule of thumb you can use is this: If a composite object is just the sum of the parts of one or more base objects, then an interface should probably be used instead of inheritance.

SUMMARY

Abstract classes and interfaces are two of the most powerful OOP tools. Using either of these methods, a programmer can define a type (class) that can be realized using multiple implementations. Determining which technique to use is not always clear to new object-oriented programmers. Joshua Bloch, in his book *Effective Java Programming Language Guide* (Bloch 2001), suggests that, in most cases, interfaces should be preferred over abstract classes. Here are his reasons:

- An existing class can more easily be modified to work with a new interface than it can to work with a new abstract class.
- Interfaces are better building blocks for nonhierarchical class frameworks since any class can implement multiple interfaces.
- Interfaces more easily enable enhancements to classes that implement them since the programmer isn't forced to use inheritance.

See Bloch's book (2001, pp. 84–88) for a more complete list and explanation of these differences.

EXERCISES

1. A point in a plane is described by its *x* and *y* coordinates. Design an abstract class that implements the concept of a point. Include method headings for setting each coordinate and displaying the coordinates individually and as a point.
2. Using the abstract class developed in Exercise 1, create a derived class that inherits from the abstract Point class and fully implements all the methods described in the abstract class.
3. Redefine the Point class as an interface.
4. Redo Exercise 2, this time implementing the class from the Point interface.

5. Derive a Circle class from the class developed in Exercise 2. A circle is defined by its center point and a radius. Write methods for working with these data members as well as methods that calculate the area and the circumference.

6. Create a Circle class that implements the interface defined in Exercise 4. Include all the methods developed in Exercise 5.

CHAPTER 7

Implementing the IEnumerable and IComparable Interfaces

Data we create via object creation cannot be treated in the same way native data (integers, strings, etc.) are treated. When we are working with strings, for example, it is easy to compare two strings to see if they are equivalent. In contrast, when we are working with two class objects, where each object is a composite of multiple data types, how we report the result of comparing the two objects is not obvious. Visual Basic.NET provides a special interface, IComparable, to aid us in making these types of comparisons.

Class objects also present a problem when we want to store them in a data structure and retrieve them using a For Each loop. The VB.NET compiler cannot automatically return an enumerator for class objects stored in an ArrayList or some other data structure, so we must provide the enumeration code. The .NET Framework again helps us in this task by providing an interface, IEnumerable, that we can implement. In this chapter we'll discuss how to implement both interfaces and provide several examples to see exactly how they're used.

THE ICOMPARABLE INTERFACE

A class type usually represents a complex data type comprising components of one of the built-in data types (String, Integer, Boolean, etc.). For example, an Employee class might include data for an employee's name (including the first, middle, and last name), social security number, salary, the department in which he or she works, etc. If we want to compare two Employee objects to see if they are the same, how do we do it? Do we compare the two objects by the strings stored in the name data members? Do we compare them by their social security numbers? Or do we compare two Employee objects by some combination of data members?

These questions become quite pertinent when we decide we need to sort a set of class objects stored in a data structures. What does the sort method use to determine the order of the objects? Again, the compiler doesn't know which of the data members is supposed to be the "key" in the sort. With the Employee class, we might want to sort the objects by name, department, or salary. We have to chose which data member to sort by through the use of the IComparable interface, through which we implement a custom CompareTo method.

The CompareTo Method

The CompareTo method compares two data objects and returns a value based on the comparison. The general form of the method is

```
rv = obj1.CompareTo(obj2)
```

where rv is a variable that stores the return value of the method.

The possible return values from the method are as follows:

- zero, if the two objects are the same;
- greater than zero if obj1 is greater than obj2; and
- less than zero if obj1 is less than obj2.

Usually, the "greater than zero" value is 1 and the "less than zero" value is −1, but these values cannot be guaranteed and you should take this into account when you write code using the CompareTo method.

As an example of how the CompareTo method works, the following code compares two strings three different times using the CompareTo method:

```
Imports System
Module CompTest
  Sub Main()
    Dim name1, name2 As String
    Dim result As Integer
    name1 = "Michael Mason McMillan"
    name2 = "Michael Mason McMillan"
    result = name1.CompareTo(name2)
    Console.WriteLine("name1: " & name1 & " name2: " & _
                      name2)
    Select Case result
      Case 0
        Console.WriteLine("name1 and name2 are equal.")
      Case Is >= 1
        Console.WriteLine("name1 is greater than name2.")
      Case Is < 1
        Console.WriteLine("name1 is less than name2.")
    End Select
    name2 = "Joel Mason McMillan"
    result = name1.CompareTo(name2)
    Console.WriteLine("name1: " & name1 & " name2: " & _
                      name2)
    Select Case result
      Case 0
        Console.WriteLine("name1 and name2 are equal.")
      Case Is >= 1
        Console.WriteLine("name1 is greater than name2.")
      Case Is < 1
        Console.WriteLine("name1 is less than name2.")
    End Select
    name2 = "Thomas Mason McMillan"
    result = name1.CompareTo(name2)
    Console.WriteLine("name1: " & name1 & " name2: " & _
                      name2)
    Select Case result
      Case 0
```

```
          Console.WriteLine("name1 and name2 are equal.")
        Case Is >= 1
          Console.WriteLine("name1 is greater than name2.")
        Case Is < 1
          Console.WriteLine("name1 is less than name2.")
      End Select
    End Sub
  End Module
```

The output from this program is

```
name1: Michael Mason McMillan   name2: Michael Mason McMillan
name1 and name2 are equal.
name1: Michael Mason McMillan   name2: Joel Mason McMillan
name1 is greater than name2.
name1: Michael Mason McMillan   name2: Thomas Mason McMillan
name1 is less than name2.
```

An alternative means of making comparisons is the Compare method, but this method is not implemented in the IComparable interface, so we won't discuss it here.

Implementing the IComparable Interface

A class that implements the IComparable interface has to do two things—specify the interface at the beginning of the class definition and implement the CompareTo method in the class definition. We've already seen how to specify an interface name at the beginning of a class definition, but here's another example:

```
Public Class Employee
    Implements IComparable

  ' Class code
End Class
```

Now we're ready to implement the CompareTo method for the class. The key to the implementation is to choose a data member we wish to use for comparisons and write the code so that the data member is used with the CompareTo method from the interface. For this discussion, we'll use the Department data member for our comparisons. This means that if we store a set of Employee objects in a data structure and sort them, the objects will be sorted alphabetically by the Department data member.

The code for the method is simple and straightforward:

```
Public Function CompareTo(ByVal obj As Object) As _
  Integer Implements IComparable.CompareTo
    Return Me.Department.CompareTo(CType(obj, Employee) _
                          .Department)
End Function
```

The method heading indicates that the argument passed to the method is of Object type and the method returns an integer. Returning an integer is the standard behavior for the CompareTo method. Although the parameter list indicates the argument to the method can be an object, the actual argument passed must be of the same type as the implementing class or an ArgumentException error will be thrown.

The body of the method consists of just one line. Since we are comparing Department data members to determine order, the Department member of the current object calls the CompareTo method for strings. Its argument is the Department member of the passed-in Employee object, which is converted from Object to Employee using the CType method.

When we implement the CompareTo method, we break a class object down to a native type that can make its own call to a CompareTo method. This is not particularly difficult to understand, since the CompareTo method for strings (or any other data type) is very well understood. We have to do this only because the class object is complex, whereas each of the constituent data members (in this example at least) comprises atomic data.

Let's look at a more complete class definition of the Employee class implementing IComparable:

```
Public Class Employee
    Implements IComparable
  Private Name As String
  Private ID As String
  Private Department As String
```

```
    Private Salary As Integer

    Public Sub New(ByVal name As String, ByVal id As _
                String, ByVal dept As String, ByVal _
                salary As Integer)
      Me.Name = name
      Me.ID = id
      Me.Department = dept
      Me.Salary = salary
    End Sub

    Public Function getName() As String
      Return Me.Name
    End Function

    Public Function getDept() As String
      Return Me.Department
    End Function

    Public Function CompareTo(ByVal obj As Object) As _
     Integer Implements IComparable.CompareTo
      Return Me.Department.CompareTo(CType(obj, _
                                    Employee).Department)
    End Function

    ' More class functionality here

End Class
```

Here's a program that tests the class:

```
Sub Main()
  Dim empList As New ArrayList()
  Dim emp1, emp2, emp3, e As Employee
  emp1 = New Employee("Jane Doe", "12345", "Finance", _
                  40000)
  emp2 = New Employee("John Smith", "34567", "IS", 42000)
  emp3 = New Employee("Mike McMillan", "11112", _
                  "Accounting", 75000)
  empList.Add(emp1)
  empList.Add(emp2)
```

```
    empList.Add(emp3)
    empList.Sort()
    For Each e In empList
        Console.WriteLine(e.getName() & ": " & e.getDept())
    Next
    Console.Read()
End Sub
```

The output from this program is:

```
Mike McMillan: Accounting
Jane Doe: Finance
John Smith: IS
```

If we want to change the comparison data member from Department to, say, Salary, all we have to do is change the method:

```
Public Function CompareTo(ByVal obj As Object) As _
  Integer Implements IComparable.CompareTo
    Return Me.Salary.CompareTo(CType(obj, Employee).Salary)
End Function
```

Creating a Custom Comparer

For many classes, a simple comparison using one of the data members of the class may not be enough. For example, in the Employee class just presented, we might want to sort the class objects by either department or salary. We can accomplish this by creating our own implementation of IComparer.

THE IENUMERABLE INTERFACE

Many programs that use class objects will want to store currently instantiated objects in a data structure of some type. Typically in OOP, a container class is created for storing class objects. A container class usually consists of nothing more than a data structure (such as an ArrayList) that is wrapped up in class code. By placing class objects in a container class we have a convenient structure for performing operations on all the same-class objects in a program.

Once we get class objects into a container class, we need a way to pull them out as a group. The standard way to perform this type of operation is to use a For Each loop. However, because our class object is not built into the language, the For Each loop cannot access a built-in enumerator object for its use. We have to provide the code for an enumerator object, as well as the code to iterate through the class objects contained in the enumerator. The container class we build must implement the IEnumerable interface to use the For Each loop with the class.

Implementing the IEnumerable Interface

There are two things we have to do when we build a container class that implements the IEnumerable interface. First, our container class must implement a GetEnumerator object that returns an enumerator for use. This enumerator is actually another implementation, this time of the IEnumerator interface. The second thing we must do is create a Private class that contains the methods used to to enumerate a set of class objects.

The container class implements the IEnumerable interface. The standard technique for implementing the IEnumerator interface is to create a private class inside the container class. That is the technique we'll use here.

In this example we're using the Employees class of the previous section. We've added just a few getter and setter methods to the class to view more data. Here's the new code for the Employee class:

```
Public Class Employee
   Private Name As String
   Private ID As String
   Private Department As String
   Private Salary As Integer

   Public Sub New(ByVal name As String, ByVal id As _
               String, ByVal dept As String, ByVal _
               salary As Integer)
     Me.Name = name
     Me.ID = id
     Me.Department = dept
     Me.Salary = salary
   End Sub
```

```
    Public Sub setName(ByVal name As String)
      Me.Name = name
    End Sub

    Public Function getName() As String
      Return Name
    End Function

    Public Sub setID(ByVal id As String)
      Me.ID = id
    End Sub

    Public Function getID() As String
      Return ID
    End Function

    Public Sub setDept(ByVal dept As String)
      Me.Department = dept
    End Sub

    Public Function getDept() As String
      Return Department
    End Function

    Public Sub setSalary(ByVal salary As Integer)
      Me.Salary = salary
    End Sub

    Public Function getSalary() As Integer
      Return Salary
    End Function

  End Class
```

Now let's look at the container class we're creating to store Employee objects. This class is named Employees, and its only private data member is an ArrayList to store objects. We don't really need a constructor for this class so we just write an empty constructor method. We need a method for returning the number of items in the container and we need a method for adding new objects to the container. Here's the class definition so far:

```
Public Class Employees
  Implements IEnumerable
```

```
    Private pEmployees As New ArrayList()

    Public Sub New()
    End Sub

    Public Function Count() As Integer
      Return pEmployees.Count
    End Function

    Public Sub AddEmployee(ByVal employee As Employee)
      pEmployees.Add(employee)
    End Sub

    ' More code to come

End Class
```

Now we need to implement the GetEnumerator method. This method returns an IEnumerator object and does this by instantiating a new Enumerator object created with a private class written only to implement the Enumerator object. The code for GetEnumerator looks like this:

```
Public Function GetEnumerator() As IEnumerator _
  Implements System.Collections.IEnumerable.GetEnumerator

    Return New EmployeeEnumerator(pEmployees)
End Function
```

This code is very straightforward and doesn't really do anything that interesting. The real work is performed inside the EmployeeEnumerator class.

This class implements the IEnumerator interface. The class has two data members: 1. an ArrayList that represents the objects in the container class and 2. a position variable that we use to keep track of the current element in the ArrayList. The position variable is initialized to -1, meaning that it must be incremented to return the first element in the ArrayList.

There are three methods that must be implemented in the EmployeeEnumerator class—Current(), MoveNext(), and Reset(). The Current() method returns the object in the current position of the ArrayList using the position variable. The MoveNext() method increments the position variable by 1 and tests to make sure that the upper bound of the ArrayList hasn't been reached.

MoveNext() is a Boolean method; it returns True if the position variable is within the bounds of the ArrayList and returns False if the value of the variable is beyond the upper bound. Finally, the Reset() method simply sets the value of the position variable back to -1.

Here's the code for the EmployeeEnumerator class:

```
Private Class EmployeeEnumerator
  Implements IEnumerator

  Private pEmployees As ArrayList
  Private position As Integer = -1

  Public Sub New(ByVal employees As ArrayList)
    pEmployees = employees
  End Sub

  ' Implementation of IEnumerator
  Public ReadOnly Property Current() As Object _
   Implements System.Collections.IEnumerator.Current

    Get
      Return pEmployees(position)
    End Get

  End Property

  ' Implementation of IEnumerator
  Public Function MoveNext() As Boolean _
   Implements System.Collections.IEnumerator.MoveNext

    position += 1

    If position >= pEmployees.Count Then
      Return False
    Else
      Return True
    End If

  End Function

  ' Implementation of IEnumerator
  Public Sub Reset() _
   Implements System.Collections.IEnumerator.Reset
```

```
      position = -1

   End Sub

End Class
```

Once we put the EmployeeEnumerator class inside the Employees class, we're ready to use the collection class in a program. Here's an example:

```
Sub main()

  Dim emps As New Employees()
  emps.AddEmployee(New Employee("Mike McMillan", _
                "1234", "Prog", 45000))
  emps.AddEmployee(New Employee("Raymond Williams", _
                "2345", "Inter", 50000))
  emps.AddEmployee(New Employee("David Durr", "5323", _
                "Netw", 27000))
  emps.AddEmployee(New Employee("Bernica Tackett", _
                "4298", "Netw", 53000))
  Dim emp As Employee
  For Each emp In emps
    Console.WriteLine("Name: " & emp.getName())
    Console.WriteLine("ID: " & emp.getID())
    Console.WriteLine("Department: " & emp.getDept())
    Console.WriteLine("Salary: " & emp.getSalary())
    Console.WriteLine()
  Next
  Console.Read()

End Sub
```

Summary

Creating classes introduces many complexities into a program. This is partly due to the data complexity of a class. Very rarely will all the data members of a class consist of the same data type. Because of this, the standard comparison operators and enumerators will not work properly on class objects. This chapter introduces the reader to two interfaces that provide the programmer with the means of creating custom comparisons and enumerators that can work with complex objects. If the objects of a class you create will be compared to each other, or you need to put your class objects into a collection, you should implement these interfaces.

EXERCISES

1. Implement the IComparable interface for the DateType class discussed earlier in the book. Test your implementation with a program that compares different DateType objects.
2. Using the DateType class again, implement the IEnumerable interface and write a program to test your implementation.
3. Create a GradeBook class that keeps track of a list of students and their grades for one course. (You may want to create a Student class also.) Implement both the IComparable interface and the IEnumerable interface in this class and write a test program to ensure that your implementation works properly.

CHAPTER 8

Designing and Implementing Exception Classes

Programs written in VB.NET utilize the Throw-Catch model of exception handling when dealing with errors. The classes found in the.NET Framework use this model for handling errors, but the classes you develop must generate their own exceptions for handling errors. In this chapter, we discuss how exception classes are created and how to use them. We start the chapter with a review of the Throw-Catch model, which includes the Try-Catch-Finally statement.

EXCEPTION HANDLING IN VB.NET

The term VB.NET uses for errors that occur in executing code is *exception*. Writing code that deals with errors in a program is called *exception handling*. Exception handling in VB.NET consists of writing code that watches for exceptions when they're thrown and writing code that causes an exception to be thrown when an error condition arises. A VB.NET programmer is not responsible for always writing exception-generating code since the.NET Framework classes throw their own exceptions.

For example, trying to open a file that doesn't exist throws an exception because there was no file to open. This object is called FileNotFoundException.

In the next section we examine how to write code to catch built-in exception objects.

Writing Exception-Handling Code

As we've discussed, trying to open a nonexistent file throws an exception. For our program to recognize the exception, we have to use a special construct—the Try-Catch-Finally statement.

The general form of the Try-Catch-Statement is as follows:

Try
    Code that might throw exception
Catch exception object as exception type
    Code to handle thrown exception
Finally
    Code to clean things up
End Try

The code that might throw an exception is placed inside the Try block of the statement. Any code that could possibly lead to an exception should be placed in this block. This means code that can generate any type of exception, so that file input/output code, arithmetic code, and so on can go in the same block. We don't have to limit ourselves to code that can throw one type of exception.

We can best demonstrate how this works with a short example. The following program attempts to open a file, read it line-by-line, and write the lines to a new file. We are worried that the file we want to open is not in the path we specify (from the command line), so we put our code in a Try-Catch block:

```
Imports System.IO
Module module1
  Sub main()
    Dim inFile As StreamReader
    Dim outFile As StreamWriter
    Dim line As String
    Dim args() As String = _
     Environment.GetCommandLineArgs
```

```
    Try
      outFile = File.CreateText(args(2))
      inFile = File.OpenText(args(1))
      While (inFile.Peek <> -1)
        line = inFile.ReadLine
        outFile.WriteLine(line)
      End While
    Catch noFile As FileNotFoundException
      Console.WriteLine(noFile.Message)
    End Try
    Console.Read()
  End Sub
End Module
```

If the file specified in the line

```
inFile = File.OpenText(args(1))
```

is not found, an exception is thrown. The exception is caught in the line

```
Catch noFile As FileNotFoundException
```

and the exception object is stored in the object noFile.

To retrieve the message generated by the exception, the Exception class provides a Message method. This method returns a basic message indicating what caused the exception to be thrown. For example, the message returned in the previous example is

```
Could not find file "c:\afile.txt"
```

You can get a message with more information by calling the ToString method instead of the Message method. The output from the ToString method for the FileNotFoundException is as follows:

```
System.IO.FileNotFoundException: Could not find file _
 "c:\afile.txt".
File name: "c:\afile.txt"
  at System.IO._Error.WinIOError(Int32 errorCode, _
                                String str)
  at System.IO.FileStream..ctor(String path, _
   FileMode mode, FileAccess access,
```

```
FileShare share, Int32 bufferSize, Boolean useAsync, _
  String msgPath, Boolean
bFromProxy)
   at System.IO.FileStream..ctor(String path, FileMode _
    mode, FileAccess access,
FileShare share, Int32 bufferSize)
   at System.IO.StreamReader..ctor(String path, _
    Encoding encoding, Boolean detect
EndCodingFromByteOrderMarks, Inte32 bufferSize)
   at System.IO.STreamReader..ctor(String path)
   at System.IO.File.OpenText(String path)
   at ConsoleApplication11.module1.main() in
c:\executables\ConsoleApplication11
\Module1.vb: line 10
```

This exception message is much more meaningful than the previous message. However, it's probably not anything you would want the user to see, so it is best to use the ToString method during testing and debugging and just use the Message method in production code.

Catching Multiple Exceptions

You are not limited to catching just one exception in a Try-Catch statement. Multiple exceptions can be handled using a sequence of Catch statements. Let's look at an example. Our program opens a file to pull in two integers to divide the first integer by the second. If the second integer (denominator) is 0, this will lead to an overflow error. (Division by zero is not allowed on integers; with doubles, the operation yields the value Infinity.)

We can write a Catch statement for this exception in two ways. We can use the more general object, ArithmeticException, or, since we know what the exception is, we can use the more specific object, OverflowException. We'll use the second object since it makes our exception handling easier to understand.

In the following, we write a first Catch statement to catch the FileNotFoundException object, and then we write another Catch statement to catch the OverflowException object. Here's the program:

```
Imports System.IO
Module module1
```

```
Sub main()
  Dim inFile As StreamReader
  Dim line As String
  Dim numer, denom, quotient As Integer
  Dim args() As String = _
   Environment.GetCommandLineArgs
  Try
    inFile = File.OpenText(args(1))
    line = inFile.ReadLine()
    numer = CInt(line)
    line = inFile.ReadLine()
    denom = CInt(line)
    quotient = numer / denom
    Console.WriteLine(numer & " divided by " & denom _
                    & " equals " & quotient)
  Catch noFile As FileNotFoundException
    Console.WriteLine(noFile.Message)
  Catch divZero As OverflowException
    Console.WriteLine(divZero.Message)
  End Try
  Console.Read()
End Sub
End Module
```

We can write as many Catch statements as we need to handle the exceptions that might be thrown by our programs.

The Finally Statement

If we want to run a block of code after all exception handling is performed, we can add a Finally statement to the Try-Catch statement. This block can be used to release resources loaded earlier in the program, display a final message to the user, or perform anything that needs to happen before the program terminates.

In the next example, the Finally statement displays a message box letting the user know that the program is about to stop. The use of the message box in a Console application is allowed and can be a great attention getter. Here's the code:

```
Imports System.IO
Module module1
  Sub main()
    Dim inFile As StreamReader
    Dim line As String
    Dim numer, denom, quotient As Integer
    Dim args() As String = _
     Environment.GetCommandLineArgs
    Try
      inFile = File.OpenText(args(1))
      line = inFile.ReadLine()
      numer = CInt(line)
      line = inFile.ReadLine()
      denom = CInt(line)
      quotient = numer / denom
      Console.WriteLine(numer & " divided by " & _
                        denom & " equals " & quotient)
    Catch noFile As FileNotFoundException
      Console.WriteLine(noFile.Message)
    Catch divZero As OverflowException
      Console.WriteLine(divZero.Message)
    Finally
      MsgBox("Program terminating.")
    End Try
    Console.Read()
  End Sub
End Module
```

A Finally statement is not required (as you've well seen) in a Try-Catch, but it can be useful for cleaning things up when your program needs to terminate prematurely because of a thrown exception.

CREATING AND USING AN EXCEPTION CLASS

You should consider designing and implementing your own exception objects for the classes you create in your programs. An exception class is relatively simple to implement because your class will inherit most of its functionality from the Exception class that is part of the.NET Framework.

Building an Exception Class

You start the design of an Exception class by inheriting from the Exception class. Next, you have to call the Base class constructor method. And that's all you have to do. Nothing, well, almost nothing, can be simpler.

Let's look at an example using the beginnings of a class that works with rational numbers. A rational number class encapsulates two integers—the numerator and the denominator. As a general rule, the denominator cannot be the value 0, since that causes the rational number's value to be Infinity (or at least on some systems). To keep this from happening, our Rational class constructor throws an exception when the denominator is set to 0.

Before we look at the class that implements the exception object, let's look at the code that throws the exception:

```
Public Class Rational

   Private numer As Integer
   Private denom As Integer

   Public Sub New(ByVal numer As Integer, ByVal denom _
                 As Integer)
     Me.numer = numer
     If (denom = 0) Then
       Throw New InvalidRational("Denominator _
                                 can't be 0.")

     Else
       Me.denom = denom
     End If
   End Sub

   ' More class code goes here

End Class
```

The constructor method throws an exception, InvalidRational, if the denominator in the argument list is 0. Now let's look at the definition for the InvalidRational class:

```
Public Class InvalidRational
   Inherits Exception
   Public Sub New(msg As String)
```

```
      MyBase.New(msg)
   End Sub
End Class
```

The message displayed when an InvalidRational exception is thrown is passed into the constructor when the object is instantiated.

This is not the only way to create an exception object. The Exception class includes a read-only property, Message, which you can override in your inherited class. Then you can retrieve the message when the exception is thrown by making a call to the property. To see how this works, let's first look at a new definition for the InvalidRational class:

```
Public Class InvalidRational
   Inherits Exception

   Private except As String = "Denominator can't be 0."

   Overrides ReadOnly Property Message() As String
     Get
        Return except
     End Get
   End Property

   Public Sub New()
     MyBase.New()
   End Sub
End Class
```

The Rational class calls the exception in the same way and the user code simply accesses the Message property to display the exception message, exactly as we did before. Here's all the code for this example in one place:

```
Imports System.IO
Module module1
   Public Class InvalidRational
     Inherits Exception

     Private except As String = "Denominator can't be 0."
     Overrides ReadOnly Property Message() As String
       Get
          Return except
       End Get
```

```
     End Property

     Public Sub New()
       MyBase.New()
     End Sub

   End Class

   Public Class Rational

     Private numer As Integer
     Private denom As Integer

     Public Sub New(ByVal numer As Integer, ByVal _
                 denom As Integer)
       Me.numer = numer
       If (denom = 0) Then
           Throw New InvalidRational()
       Else
         Me.denom = denom
       End If
     End Sub

   End Class

   Sub main()

     Try
       Dim rat1 As New Rational(3, 0)
     Catch badRat As InvalidRational
         Console.WriteLine(badRat.Message)
     End Try
     Console.Read()

   End Sub

 End Module
```

SUMMARY

Exceptions provide a structured means of handling errors in programs. They are a vast improvement over the On Error–GoTo construct found in previous versions of Visual Basic.

When you create your own classes, you will need to also create an exception class if you want the object to throw exceptions. An exception class is easy to create and has a minimum of components. Most users of custom classes expect the class to include exception handling as part of the interface.

One final word of warning needs to be issued about exceptions: Use them only for exceptional situations. As you have seen, using exception handling modifies the normal control of flow of a program and can lead to very messy code. Many situations where exceptions are often used, such as going past the upper bound of an array or checking the status of a file, are not really exceptional and should be handled with other constructs that aren't so potentially confusing.

EXERCISES

1. In an earlier chapter you developed a class that functions as a bounded counter. Create a Clock class (an example of a bounded counter) that includes an Exception class that throws exceptions if the minutes or seconds are incremented to 61, instead of back to 1. Write a program to test your implementation.
2. Create a DateType class (or use an earlier implementation). Add an Exception class that throws exceptions if an invalid date is stored. We will leave it to your imagination to decide just what constitutes an invalid date, but you know things such as a month with 32 days or February 29 in a nonleap year are invalid dates.

CHAPTER 9

Design Patterns and Refactoring

It is not enough just to know how to write object-oriented programs; you also have to know how to write object-oriented programs well. As you gain experience writing object-oriented programs, you will discover certain programming idioms that are used over and over again. These idioms are called design patterns.

DESIGN PATTERNS

Design patterns were first described in *Design Patterns—Elements of Reusable Object-Oriented Software* (Gamma 1995). A design pattern is a solution to a recurring problem in object-oriented design and implementation. There are four parts to a design pattern, as described in Gamma et al.'s book (Gamma 1995, p. 3):

- Pattern name—A name for making it easier to discuss using the pattern.
- Problem—An explanation of the problem and its context.
- Solution—An abstract description of the design problem and how to use VB.NET code to solve it.
- Consequences—The pros and cons of implementing the design pattern.

The Shared Factory Method

Using constructors to create instances of classes is not always the preferred approach to instantiating class objects. One problem with constructors is that they don't have names, which can lead to confusing code. Another problem with constructors is that each constructor has to have its own signature, meaning that only one type of class object can be instantiated for each signature.

We can work around these problems by writing methods that create objects. This is a design pattern known as a factory method. In this case, we create a Shared Factory method that can be called without needing an instance of a class.

Internally, we still make a constructor call because VB.NET requires one to create an object. However, we can declare the constructor as a Private method so that it can only be called internally.

To demonstrate how a Shared Factory method works, we can write the following code to use the method to create instance of its type:

```
Public Class DateType

  Private month As Integer
  Private day As Integer
  Private year As Integer

  Private Sub New()
    month = 0
    day = 0
    year = 0
  End Sub

  Public Shared Function valueOf(d As DateType) As _
   DateType
    d.month = Now.Month
    d.day = Now.Day
    d.year = Now.Year
    Return d
  End Function

  Public Sub Display()
    Console.WriteLine(month & "/" & day & "/" & year)
  End Sub

End Class
```

A DateType object is created like this:

```
Sub Main()
  Dim today As DateType
  today = DateType.valueOf(today)
  today.Display()
  Console.Read()
End Sub
```

There are problems with using the Shared Factory method. First, a class created this way cannot be inherited because the class won't have a Public constructor. This is not necessarily a bad thing since programmers are encouraged to favor composition (i.e., interfaces) over inheritance anyway.

A second problem with using Shared Factory methods is that they cannot be easily distinguished from other methods because they are not labeled with easily understood names (such as New for a constructor method).

Bloch (Bloch 2001, pp. 5–9) discusses the Shared Factory method in some detail.

The Singleton Pattern

A very common design pattern in OOP is the *singleton* pattern. A singleton is a class that only allows one instance of its type during the lifetime of a program. Singletons are used in many different types of programs. For instance, an operating system just has one file system object, just as it has only one print spooler object. A singleton pattern ensures that when a class is exposed in a program, the user will only be able to create one instance of the class.

As with the Shared Factory pattern, the key to the singleton pattern is to make the constructor method Private. A Private constructor method makes it impossible for client code to instantiate an object of the class. The singleton pattern uses a technique for creating a single instance that is similar to how the Shared Factory method creates objects. Let's look at the code for the class and then discuss exactly how it creates just a single instance. The following example defines a class for making connections to databases. The actual code for doing that is left out. We examine database applications later in the book. Here's the code:

```
Public Class DBConnection

  Private Shared Instance As DBConnection
  Private Shared created As Boolean = False
  Public check As String' This is just for testing _
   purposes

  Private Sub New()
    ' No code needed here
  End Sub

  Public Shared Function getInstance() As DBConnection
    If (Not (created)) Then
      Instance = New DBConnection()
      created = True
      Return Instance
    Else
      Return Instance
    End If
  End Function

End Class
```

There are two data members in the class: Instance, the DBConnection object, and created, a Boolean variable we use to determine if an instance of the class has already been created or not. The other variable, check, is there simply to use as a test. We'll get back to that variable later.

Because the constructor method is declared as a Private method, there is no chance that user code will make a constructor call. All the work is performed in the getInstance function. The function first checks the created variable for a True or False value. If the value is True, then an instance has already been created and the function just returns the same instance. If the value is False, then a new instance is created and stored in the variable Instance. The created variable is set to True and the instance is returned.

The following code shows how we can test to see if the singleton pattern is working:

```
Sub Main()
  Dim myconn As DBConnection
  myconn = DBConnection.getInstance()
```

```
    myconn:check = "Testing, testing, testing"
    Console.WriteLine("Value of check: " & myconn.check)
    Dim anotherconn As DBConnection
    anotherconn = DBConnection.getInstance()
    Console.WriteLine("Should match above: " & _
                    anotherconn.check)
    Console.Read()
  End Sub
```

The output from this program is

```
  Value of check: Testing, testing, testing
  Should match above: Testing, testing, testing
```

Clearly, the second instance of DBConnection is the same as the first instance.

REFACTORING

The concept of *refactoring* was introduced in Martin Fowler's book, *Refactoring—Improving the Design of Existing Code* (Fowler 2000). Refactoring refers to making changes to the code in a program to make it easier to understand and easier to modify without actually changing the behavior of the program (Fowler 2000, p. 53). Refactoring is not strictly an OOP technique, but it is usually considered as part of the OOP toolbox because the concept was first touted by Smalltalk, C++, and Java programmers.

When many experienced programmers first hear about refactoring, they say "Well, I've been doing that all along." And, indeed, the best programmers have always used refactoring in their programming practice. So what is refactoring, exactly?

In one sense, refactoring is simply cleaning up your code. The canonical example of refactoring involves taking a segment of code that is used over and over again and turning it into a method. Every programmer has done this type of refactoring many, many times. A change like this makes the code easier both to read and to modify, but it doesn't change the behavior of the program, since the method definition contains the code segment that was being used.

But this is just one type of refactoring. Fowler provides a catalog of over seventy named refactorings. There are refactorings for extracting classes from code, changing a group of parameters to a parameter object, moving constructors in subclasses to a constructor in the base class, and performing many more tasks. We will examine several of these and other refactorings later in this section. First, we need to examine what refactoring does for our programs.

The Benefits of Refactoring

Fowler lists several reasons why refactoring should be used with all programming projects (Fowler 2000, pp. 55–57). These reasons include the following:

- **Improving software design.** As the coding on a program progresses, the design of the program degrades. Changes made to the code cause it to lose its structure. Refactoring helps the code regain its structure. Also, as the design degrades, the program will take on more code, often doing the same things. Refactoring helps to get rid of duplicate code.

- **Making software easier to understand.** First, refactoring makes complicated code easier to understand. This much should be obvious to any experienced programmer. Refactoring can also help you understand unfamiliar code. When you read code with an eye toward refactoring, you read the code at a different level than when you are just trying to understand what it does.

- **Finding bugs.** Refactoring forces you to concentrate on code in a way you probably don't when you are just reviewing code. A better understanding of a piece of code will help you discover where the bugs are in that code.

- **Increasing programming speed.** Refactoring leads to a better software design. A good software design, in turn, leads to faster development. A good design allows you to focus on adding new functionality to the program and not on constantly chasing down bugs.

Refactoring Examples

This section discusses several refactoring examples, starting with some simple examples and moving to more complex refactorings. Many of them are based on OOP, but not all of them are. These examples will use the names in Fowler's book (Fowler 2000).

Extract Method

This is one of the most basic refactorings and one that all programmers, especially programmers with one or two larger programs under their belt, have performed. You notice in your program a particular code segment that is used over and over again. This segment should be turned into a method.

The next example demonstrates a simple use of an Extract method. A Windows form has a button that is used to clear input from text boxes. It is tempting to just write the code like this:

```
Private Sub btnClear_Click(. . .). . .
  TextBox1.Text = ""
  TextBox2.Text = ""
  TextBox3.Text = ""
  TextBox4.Text = ""
End Sub
```

But you may want to call this code segment in many other places, so you build a method:

```
Private Sub ClearTextBoxes()
  TextBox1.Text = ""
  TextBox2.Text = ""
  TextBox3.Text = ""
  TextBox4.Text = ""
End Sub
```

Now the code in the button's Click event looks like this:

```
Private Sub btnClear_Click(. . .). . .
  ClearTextBoxes()
End Sub
```

Although this example is quite simple, it begins to show the power of refactoring. Let's look at another Extract method example that is a bit more complex.

The following class keeps track of grades in a college course. The class consists of just two data members, a constructor, and two methods—one for setting the grades and one for showing the average test grade. Here's the original code:

```
Public Class Grades

  Private gradebook() As Integer
  Private pos As Integer

  Public Sub New(ByVal numElements As Integer)
    ReDim gradebook(numElements)
    pos = 0
  End Sub

  Public Sub setGrade(ByVal grade As Integer)
    gradebook(pos) = grade
    pos += 1
  End Sub

  Public Sub ShowGradeAverage()
    Dim total, grade As Integer
    Dim avg As Double
    Console.WriteLine("**************")
    Console.WriteLine("** Average ***")
    Console.WriteLine("**************")
    For Each grade In gradebook
      total += grade
    Next
    avg = total / gradebook.Length
    Console.WriteLine("Average: " & avg)
  End Sub

End Class
```

The ShowGradeAverage method can use some refactoring. Clearly, we can write a method to print the banner and we can write another method to calculate the average grade. The banner method may not be needed again, but we might need to use the calculating method again. Here's the new class definition after the refactorings:

```
Public Class Grades

  Private gradebook() As Integer
  Private pos As Integer
```

```vbnet
Public Sub New(ByVal numElements As Integer)
  ReDim gradebook(numElements)
  pos = 0
End Sub

Public Sub setGrade(ByVal grade As Integer)
  gradebook(pos) = grade
  pos += 1
End Sub

Public Sub ShowGradeAverage()
  Dim avgGrade As Double
  PrintHeading()
  avgGrade = CalcAverage()
  Console.WriteLine("Average: " & avgGrade)
End Sub

Private Sub PrintHeading()
  Console.WriteLine("**************")
  Console.WriteLine("** Average ***")
  Console.WriteLine("**************")
End Sub

Private Function CalcAverage() As Double
  Dim total, grade As Integer
  Dim avg As Double
  For Each grade In gradebook
    total += grade
  Next
  avg = total / gradebook.Length
  Return avg
End Function

End Class
```

The ShowGradeAverage method definition is now slimmed down from ten lines of code to four lines. The calculation of the grade average has moved from the ShowGradeAverage method to its own method, CalcAverage. This is important if we want to adhere to the rule that a method should only serve one purpose. The refactoring has made the code easier to read and understand.

The only change we might want to make is to add a parameter to the CalcAverage method to pass in the array we want to use in the calculation. This isn't necessary for this program, but it improves the generality of the method. Here's the new definition:

```
Private Function CalcAverage(ByVal arr() As Integer)_
  As Double
    Dim total, grade As Integer
    Dim avg As Double
    For Each grade In arr
      total += grade
    Next
    avg = total / gradebook.Length
    Return avg
End Function
```

We also need to change the ShowGradeAverage method to reflect this new definition:

```
Sub showGradeAverage()
    Dim avgGrade As Double
    PrintHeading()
    avgGrade = CalcAverage(gradebook)
    Console.WriteLine("Average: " & avgGrade)
End Sub
```

Again, it's important to stress that we haven't changed the behavior of the Grades class at all during these refactorings. What we have accomplished, though, is to make the code easier to read, to understand, and to change and maintain.

Extract Class

The Extract Class method is used when you have a class performing operations that should be performed by another class. How do you determine when this occurs? Fowler states that when a subset of data and a subset of methods seem to go together, it is probably time to consider splitting the class (Fowler 2000, p. 149).

Here's an example of a class that will benefit from the Extract Class refactoring. The AddressBook class contains data for a name and a complete address.

There are several methods, however, that do nothing but support operations on the name. Here's the code:

```
Public Class Addressbook
   Private FirstName As String
   Private LastName As String
   Private Address As String
   Private City As String
   Private State As String
   Private ZipCode As String .

   Public Sub New(ByVal first As String, ByVal last _
               As String, ByVal addr As String, _
               ByVal cty As String, ByVal st As _
               String, ByVal zip As String)
     FirstName = first
     LastName = last
     Address = addr
     City = cty
     State = st
     ZipCode = zip
   End Sub

   Public Sub ShowFirstLast()
     Console.WriteLine(FirstName & " " & LastName)
   End Sub

   Public Sub ShowLastFirst()
     Console.WriteLine(LastName & ", " & FirstName)
   End Sub

   Public Sub ShowAddress()
     Console.WriteLine(Address)
     Console.WriteLine(City & ", " & State & " " & _
                     ZipCode)
   End Sub

End Class
```

We can extract the two name data members and the ShowFirstLast and ShowLastFirst methods out of the AddressBook class and create a Name class with them as follows:

```
Public Class Addressbook
   Private Name As Name
   Private Address As String
   Private City As String
   Private State As String
   Private ZipCode As String

   Public Sub New(ByVal first As String, ByVal last _
                As String, ByVal addr As String, _
                ByVal cty As String, ByVal st As _
                String, ByVal zip As String)
      Name = New Name(first, last)
      Address = addr
      City = cty
      State = st
      ZipCode = zip
   End Sub

   Private Sub ShowAddress()
      Console.WriteLine(Address)
      Console.WriteLine(City & ", " & State & " " & _
                ZipCode)
   End Sub

   Public Sub ShowEntry()
      Name.ShowFirstLast()
      ShowAddress()
   End Sub

End Class

Public Class Name

   Private FirstName As String
   Private LastName As String

   Public Sub New(ByVal first As String, ByVal last _
                As String)
      FirstName = first
      LastName = last
   End Sub
```

```
Public Sub ShowFirstLast()
  Console.WriteLine(FirstName & " " & LastName)
End Sub

  Public Sub ShowLastFirst()
  Console.WriteLine(LastName & ", " & FirstName)
  End Sub

End Class
```

One question we have about this refactoring deals with the access level we want to provide to the Name class. We chose here to make it a public class, but we could have just as easily chosen to make it a private class and limit its accessibility to the internals of the AddressBook class. One of the exercises at the end of the chapter provides you with just such an opportunity.

Hide the Delegate

One of the primary goals of OOP is data hiding, or encapsulation. Encapsulation allows us to design programs of objects where any one object has only minimal knowledge of how the other objects work. This ensures that our program won't easily break when we change the behavior of the objects or add objects or extract objects.

In designing an object-oriented program, we find ourselves violating the principle of encapsulation by requiring that objects have too much knowledge of other objects. Take as an example the AddressBook class from the previous section. If we want client code to have access to a name stored in an AddressBook object, we have to provide a method in the AddressBook class that returns a Name object, and then call the method that displays the name the way we want:

```
Public Class Addressbook
  ' Same code as before
  . . .

  Public Function GetName() As Name
    Return Me.Name
  End Function

End Class
```

The Name class looks exactly as it did before. Now the client code to display a name in first–last order looks like this:

```
anEntry.getName.ShowFirstLast()
```

This code exposes too much information about how the Name class works. What we want to do here is hide the Name class from the client, since the Name class is really just a helper class in this scenario. We can achieve this by adding a method to the AddressBook class:

```
Public Sub ShowName()
  Console.WriteLine(Me.Name.GetFirst & " " & _
                    Me.Name.GetLast())
End Sub
```

To make this work, we also need two accessor methods in the Name class:

```
Public Function GetFirst() As String
  Return FirstName
End Sub

Public Function GetLast() As String
  Return LastName
End Sub
```

The client can now access the name directly:

```
anEntry.ShowName()
```

Self-Encapsulated Field

There is a continuing controversy over how data members should be accessed inside their class definition. The conservative viewpoint is to provide accessor methods and only access data member values via those methods. The more carefree viewpoint is to just access the data member values directly.

One benefit to using accessor methods is that you can override these methods in derived classes if the new class requires it. An accessor method used within a class definition is an example of indirect data member access and is called self-encapsulation.

Let's look at an example using the GradeRange class:

```
Public Class GradeRange

    Private low As Integer
    Private high As Integer

    Public Sub New(ByVal low As Integer, ByVal high As _
                   Integer)
      Me.low = low
      Me.high = high
    End Sub

    Public Function Pass(ByVal arg As Integer) As Boolean
      Return (arg >= low) And (arg <= high)
    End Function

End Class
```

We make the data members self-encapsulating by providing them with access methods, both for getting and for setting. The new class definition looks like this:

```
Public Class GradeRange

    Private low As Integer
    Private high As Integer

    Public Sub New(ByVal low As Integer, ByVal high As _
                   Integer)
      Me.low = low
      Me.high = high
    End Sub

    Public Sub SetLow(ByVal arg As Integer)
      low = arg
    End Sub

    Public Function GetLow() As Integer
      Return low
    End Function

    Public Sub SetHigh(ByVal arg As Integer)
      high = arg
    End Sub
```

```
Public Function GetHigh() As Integer
   Return high
End Function

Public Function Pass(ByVal arg As Integer) As Boolean
   Return (arg >= GetLow()) And (arg <= GetHigh())
End Function

End Class
```

The advantage of providing self-encapsulated data members becomes evident when you derive a class from the base class. The accessor methods will make it easier to override the base class behavior in the derived class:

```
Public Class ReallyHardTest
   Inherits GradeRange

   Private NewLow As Integer

   Public Sub New(ByVal low As Integer, ByVal high As _
                  Integer, newLow as Integer))
     MyBase.New(low, high)
     Me.NewLow = newLow
   End Sub

   Public Function GetNewLow() As Integer
      Return NewLow
   End Function

   Public Overrides Function GetLow() As Integer
      Return Math.Max(MyBase.GetLow(), GetNewLow())
   End Function

End Class
```

Of course, creating self-encapsulated data members should be performed anytime a class is going to be a base class.

Replace an Array with an Object

In Visual Basic, unlike most other programming languages, an array can hold objects of different data types by declaring the array to be of type Object. For example, a student's four test grades can be stored in an Object array with the name being stored in the first element and the grades stored in the next four elements. The problem with this is that it's hard to remember exactly what position each name will be in when the array begins to fill up.

A refactoring solution to this problem is to replace the array with an object. First, let's look at a conventional solution to the problem mentioned in the previous paragraph:

```
Sub Main()
  Dim grades() As Object = {"Jones", 86, 64, _
                            "Smith", 94, 83}
  Dim avg As Double
  Dim last, index, total As Integer
  last = grades.GetUpperBound(0)
  For index = 0 To last Step 3
    total = grades(index + 1) + grades(index + 2)
    avg = total / 2
    Console.WriteLine(grades(index) & " average: " & _
                      avg)
  Next
End Sub
```

It's not that this code is terribly hard to read, but it could get confusing if we had considerable data in the array or had to do more complex processing on the data in the array. To use a class to solve this problem, we start out by creating a class:

```
Public Class Grades
. . .
End Class
```

Rather than store the data in an array, since each class instance will be a different student, we can just use plain data members to store the data:

```
Private name As String
Private Grade1 As Integer
Private Grade2 As Integer
```

Next we need a constructor:

```
Public Sub New(ByVal Name As String)
  Me.Name = Name
End Sub
```

We could also set the grades in the constructor, but we'll keep things simple since we need accessor methods anyway. Moreover, in real life, a Grades object will probably be instantiated before any grades are ready to be entered. (Of course, one might be writing the complete program a day or two, if not hours, before final grades were due.)

Next come the accessor methods:

```
Public Sub SetGrade1(ByVal arg As Integer)
  Grade1 = arg
End Sub

Public Function GetGrade1() As Integer
  Return Grade1
End Function

Public Sub SetGrade2(ByVal arg As Integer)
  Grade2 = arg
End Sub

Public Function GetGrade2() As Integer
  Return Grade2
End Function
```

Finally, we write a method to compute the average of the two grades:

```
Public Function Average() As Double
  Return ((GetGrade1() + GetGrade2()) / 2)
End Function
```

(And, yes, we do practice what we preach. Notice the use of the accessor methods in the Average method computation!)

We can now write some client code that uses the class. We put the code after the original program in this section that used the array:

```
Sub Main()

  ' Old, procedural code
  Dim grades() As Object = {"Jones", 86, 64, _
                            "Smith", 94, 83}
  Dim avg As Double
  Dim last, index, total As Integer
```

```
last = grades.GetUpperBound(0)
For index = 0 To last Step 3
  total = grades(index + 1) + grades(index + 2)
  avg = total / 2
  Console.WriteLine(grades(index) & " average: " & _
                    avg)
Next

' New, OOP code
Dim smith As New Grades("Smith")
Dim jones As New Grades("Jones")
smith.SetGrade1(86)
smith.SetGrade2(100)
jones.SetGrade1(77)
jones.SetGrade2(85)
Console.WriteLine("Smith average: " & smith.Average())
Console.WriteLine("Jones average: " & jones.Average())

Console.Read()

End Sub
```

We're biased, of course, but we like the look of the second code segment much better than the first segment. There aren't a lot of variables milling about, making the code look messy. Moreover, we don't have to try to play array-indexing tricks as we did in the For loop. The OOP code looks cleaner, is easier to understand, and conveys the sense of the program as well, if not better, than the procedural code.

To wrap up this example, we could write this program using an array to store the Grades objects. Here's how to do it:

```
Sub Main()

  Dim index As Integer
  Dim cis1504(1) As Grades
  cis1504(0) = New Grades("Smith")
  cis1504(0).SetGrade1(84)
  cis1504(0).SetGrade2(89)
  cis1504(1) = New Grades("Jones")
  cis1504(1).SetGrade1(93)
```

```
    cis1504(1).SetGrade2(85)
    For index = 0 To cis1504.GetUpperBound(0)
      Console.WriteLine(cis1504(index).GetName & " _
                        average: " & _
                        cis1504(index).Average)
    Next
    Console.Read()

  End Sub
```

SUMMARY

Although the two subjects of this chapter—design patterns and refactoring—are not really related, they are both considered important techniques in the OOP world. Design patterns are important because once you learn how to recognize when to use them, they can save you time and effort. Think of design patterns as high-level code reuse. Just as you often use the same lines of code over and over again (through the use of subroutines and functions), so do you use the same design patterns many times in your programs. Rather than always going back and reinventing the wheel, recognizing that a particular programming scenario calls for a certain design pattern will allow you to move past most of the conceptual design and get right to coding.

Once you've done all that coding, refactoring will help you clean up what you've written. Programmers very rarely write perfect code the first time through a program. Going back over a function or even a complete class definition and making improvements to the code makes the code more efficient and easier to maintain. You might also catch subtle errors that didn't show up initially.

EXERCISES

1. Design a TimeType class (to keep track of the system time) that utilizes the singleton pattern.
2. One use of the Shared Factory method is to provide a class with multiple constructors when two or more constructors need to share the same signature. Think of a class that needs these types of constructors and provide an implementation of the class.

3. In the Extract method section, a Name class was created with public access. Make the class Private without changing the behavior of the program.
4. You are a lab assistant in the programming lab at your school. One of the students in the introductory programming class shows you a program that stores employee records (name, id, salary) in an array. Because the data types of the employee record are different, the student had to use an Object array. Show the student a better way to store the employee records and demonstrate your expertise by writing a test program that averages the salaries of at least five employees.

CHAPTER 10

Object Internals: Reflection and Attributes

$\mathbf{R}$eflection refers to the ability of a VB.NET program to access the metadata stored in both running and existing assemblies. Using these metadata, you can examine the contents of a program, manipulate the metadata in the assembly, and even dynamically create and execute objects at runtime. Reflection allows us to dynamically invoke class member functions and even instantiate class objects dynamically.

Attributes are custom-written metadata you can add to an existing assembly. Attributes are used for several purposes:

- to indicate whether a class is serializable (see Chapter 13 for information on what this means);
- to indicate individual class fields that are not serializable;
- to perform conditional compilation; and
- to create strongly named types.

Attributes are created as classes that inherit from the System.Attribute class. Attributes are accessed using reflection, so these two topics build on each other.

USING REFLECTION

As we've already stated, reflection allows us to examine the metadata found in our VB.NET programs. To use reflection, we have to import the System. Reflection class into our application. From there, we have to decide which assembly we want to inspect and which metadata we want to look at in the assembly.

Returning Metadata from an Assembly

Assembly metadata can be returned from assemblies that exist on a machine and assemblies that are currently running on a machine. An assembly's metadata are stored in the assembly's manifest, either in a PE (portable executable) file with the MSIL code for the assembly or in a standalone PE file.

The Assembly class contains the methods we need to view assembly metadata. This class consists of a large set of methods for obtaining metadata from VB.NET assemblies. The code below demonstrates how to return basic metadata concerning an assembly:

```
Imports System.Reflection
Module Module1
  Sub Main()
    Dim myAssembly As System.Reflection.Assembly = _
     System.Reflection.Assembly.GetExecutingAssembly
    Console.WriteLine("Code base = " & myAssembly. _
                CodeBase)
    Console.WriteLine("Entry point = " & myAssembly. _
                EntryPoint.Name)
    Console.WriteLine()
    Console.WriteLine("Full name = " & myAssembly. _
                FullName)
    Console.WriteLine()
    Dim asmName As AssemblyName = myAssembly.GetName
    Console.WriteLine("Simple name = " & asmName.Name)
    Console.WriteLine()
    Dim asmVer As System.Version = asmName.Version
    Console.WriteLine("Major version = " & asmVer.Major)
    Console.WriteLine("Minor Version = " & asmVer.Minor)
    Console.WriteLine("Build version = " & asmVer.Build)
```

```
      Dim refAs As AssemblyName() = myAssembly. _
       GetReferencedAssemblies
      Dim refA As AssemblyName
      For Each refA In refAs
        Console.Write(refA.Name & " ")
      Next
      Console.Read()
    End Sub

End Module
```

USING REFLECTION WITH CLASS OBJECTS

We've limited our use of reflection in this chapter so far to returning information about assembly metadata. This is a book, however, on object-oriented programming, so it would be nice if we can use reflection with objects. And it turns out we can!

The NumberRange Class

We need a class to reflect upon, so we'll use the NumberRange class. This class allows us to easily check to see if a number is in a specified range. Here's its definition:

```
Public Class NumberRange
   Private lowValue As Double
   Private highValue As Double
   Public Sub New(ByVal low As Integer, ByVal high As _
                  Integer)
     lowValue = low
     highValue = high
   End Sub

   Public Property Low() As Double
     Get
       Return lowValue
     End Get
     Set(ByVal Value As Double)
       lowValue = Value
     End Set
```

```
End Property

Public Property High() As Double
  Get
    Return highValue
  End Get
  Set(ByVal Value As Double)
    highValue = Value
  End Set
End Property

Public Function InRange(ByVal number As Double) As _
  Boolean
  If (number >= lowValue And number <= highValue)
   Then
     Return True
  Else
     Return False
  End If
End Function

End Class
```

Retrieving Class Members

Every part of a class can be inspected using reflection. Let's start by returning all the members of the class to see what we have. To reflect on a class, we have to start by creating a Type object by calling the GetType method with a class name as the argument:

```
Dim classType as System.Type = GetType(NumberRange)
```

Next we need to create a MemberInfo object to store metadata from the NumberRange class. To do this, we need to call the GetMembers method from the Type object classType. Calling GetMembers without any parameters returns only the Public members of a class:

```
Dim members As MemberInfo() = classType.GetMembers()
```

We can then retrieve the different members by writing the following code fragment:

```
Dim member As MemberInfo
For Each member In members
  Console.WriteLine("{0}: " & " " & "{1}", member.Name,
member.MemberType)
Next
Console.Read()
```

The output from this fragment is

```
GetHashCode: Method
Equals: Method
ToString: Method
get_Low: Method
set_Low: Method
get_High: Method
set_High: Method
InRange: Method
GetType: Method
.ctor: Constructor
Low: Property
High: Property
```

This output includes both built-in methods that are part of every class and the methods we defined specifically for the NumberRange class.

Notice that the Private data members lowValue and highValue are not listed in the output. That's because, as we said, the GetMembers method returns only Public members. To retrieve Private members, as well as other access types, you have to pass a BindingFlags parameter to the method. This parameter enumerates the different ways to search and retrieve class members.

The different enumeration values you can use include the following:

- CreateInstance—An instance of the specified type is to be created.
- DeclaredOnly—Inherited members are ignored.
- Default—No binding flag is set.
- GetField—The specified field is to be returned.
- GetProperty—The specified property is to be returned.
- InvokeMethod—A particular method is to be invoked.
- Public/NonPublic—Only public and nonpublic members are returned.
- SetField—The value of the specified field is to be set.
- SetProperty—The value of the specified property is to be set.
- Static/Instance—Only static and instance members are returned.

We can use these bindings to retrieve all the members of the NumberRange class, like this:

```
Dim members As MemberInfo() = _
    classType.GetMembers(BindingFlags.Public Or
    BindingFlags.NonPublic Or _
    BindingFlags.Static Or _
    BindingFlags.Instance Or _
    BindingFlags.DeclaredOnly)
```

The output now looks like this

```
lowValue: Field
highValue: Field
get_Low: Method
set_Low: Method
get_High: Method
set_High: Method
InRange: Method
.ctor: Constructor
Low: Property
High: Property
```

Now we only see those members that are part of the definition we wrote for the class. In other words, the built-in methods are not included in this output.

Working with Class Metadata

Once we've retrieved a class's metadata into a Type object, we can use the data in many ways. The Reflection class includes classes for examining field metadata, property metadata, method metadata, constructor metadata, event metadata, and parameter metadata. In this section, we examine just a few of the many ways to work with these metadata.

When we are examining a class via reflection, there are many important properties about the class we need to discover before we can safely work with the class dynamically. For example, if we are going to invoke a class method at runtime, we'll have to know about the parameters of that method. How many parameters are there? What are their types? What are their positions in the parameter list? Likewise, there are many questions we can ask about class methods: Is the method a constructor? Is the method a shared method? What is the method's return type? These questions, and many others, can be answered by examining the metadata returned from the MethodInfo class.

Let's begin by looking at some code that examines the NumberRange class's data members (fields). The following program provides some basic information about the fields in the class:

```
Sub Main()
  Dim grades As New NumberRange(0, 100)
  Dim classType As Type = GetType(NumberRange)
  Dim numRangeFields() As FieldInfo
  numRangeFields = classType.GetFields _
                    (BindingFlags.NonPublic Or _
                     BindingFlags.Instance Or _
                     BindingFlags.Public)
  Dim index As Integer
  For index = 0 To numRangeFields.GetUpperBound(0)
    Console.WriteLine("Field name: " & _
                    numRangeFields(index).Name)
    Console.WriteLine("Declaring type: {0}", _
                    numRangeFields(index) _
                    .DeclaringType)
    Console.WriteLine("Public field?: " & _
                    numRangeFields(index).IsPublic)
    Console.WriteLine("Member type: {0}", _
                    numRangeFields(index).MemberType)
    Console.WriteLine("Field type: {0}", _
                    numRangeFields(index).FieldType)
    Console.WriteLine("Family level access: " & _
                    numRangeFields(index).IsFamily)
    Console.WriteLine()
  Next
  Console.Read()

End Sub
```

The output from this program is

```
Field name: lowValue
Declaring type: ConsoleApplication144.Module1+NumberRange
```

```
Public field?: False
Member type: Field
Field type: System.Double
Family level access: False

Field name: highValue
Declaring type: _
 ConsoleApplication144.Module1+NumberRange
Public field?: False
Member type: Field
Field type: System.Double
Family level access: False
```

We can get the same metadata on properties and methods. Since the techniques are similar, we'll just show the code for returning metadata about the methods in the NumberRange class:

```
Sub Main()
  Dim grades As New NumberRange(0, 100)
  Dim classType As Type = GetType(NumberRange)
  Dim numRangeMethods() As MethodInfo
  numRangeMethods = classType.GetMethods _
                    (BindingFlags.NonPublic Or _
                     BindingFlags.Instance Or _
                     BindingFlags.Public)
  Dim index As Integer
  For index = 0 To numRangeMethods.GetUpperBound(0)
    Console.WriteLine("Method name: " & _
                    numRangeMethods(index).Name)
    Console.WriteLine("Declaring type: {0}", _
                    numRangeMethods(index). _
                    DeclaringType)
    Console.WriteLine("Public method?: " & _
                    numRangeMethods(index).IsPublic)
    Console.WriteLine("Member type: {0}", _
                    numRangeMethods(index).MemberType)
    Console.WriteLine("Is overridable: {0}", _
                    numRangeMethods(index).IsVirtual)
```

```
        Console.WriteLine("Is a constructor: " & _
                        numRangeMethods(index). _
                        IsConstructor)
        Console.WriteLine()
    Next
    Console.Read()

End Sub
```

The output from this code is interesting because it includes some methods that are automatically created when you create a class. See if you recognize them in the following list:

```
Method name: Finalize
Declaring type: System.Object
Public method?: False
Member type: Method
Is overridable: True
Is a constructor: False

Method name: GetHashCode
Declaring type: System.Object
Public method?: True
Member type: Method
Is overridable: True
Is a constructor: False

Method name: Equals
Declaring type: System.Object
Public method?: True
Member type: Method
Is overridable: True
Is a constructor: False

Method name: ToString
Declaring type: System.Object
Public method?: True
Member type: Method
Is overridable: True
```

```
Is a constructor: False

Method name: get_Low
Declaring type: ConsoleApplication144.Module1+NumberRange
Public method?: True
Member type: Method
Is overridable: False
Is a constructor: False

Method name: set_Low
Declaring type: ConsoleApplication144.Module1+NumberRange
Public method?: True
Member type: Method
Is overridable: False
Is a constructor: False

Method name: get_High
Declaring type: ConsoleApplication144.Module1+NumberRange
Public method?: True
Member type: Method
Is overridable: False
Is a constructor: False

Method name: set_High
Declaring type: ConsoleApplication144.Module1+NumberRange
Public method?: True
Member type: Method
Is overridable: False
Is a constructor: False

Method name: InRange
Declaring type: ConsoleApplication144.Module1+NumberRange
Public method?: True
Member type: Method
Is overridable: False
Is a constructor: False

Method name: GetType
Declaring type: System.Object
Public method?: True
Member type: Method
```

```
Is overridable: False
Is a constructor: False

Method name: MemberwiseClone
Declaring type: System.Object
Public method?: False
Member type: Method
Is overridable: False
Is a constructor: False
```

As a final example of retrieving class metadata, we'll examine the parameters of a class method. We'll find this technique useful in the next section when we dynamically invoke a method. To do this properly, we'll need to know how many parameters a method takes, as well as their data type. We can retrieve this information using reflection.

The ParameterInfo class lets us retrieve metadata about a given method. First, let's look at a particular method from the NumberRange class, the In-Range method:

```
Public Function InRange(ByVal number As Double) As Boolean
  If (number >= lowValue And number <= highValue) Then
    Return True
  Else
    Return False
  End If
End Function
```

The following code returns some of the metadata stored for this method:

```
numRangeMethod = classType.GetMethod _
                ("InRange", BindingFlags.Public _
                Or BindingFlags.NonPublic Or _
                BindingFlags.Instance)
Dim methodParams() As ParameterInfo = numRangeMethod. _
                                GetParameters()
Dim index As Integer
For index = 0 To methodParams.GetUpperBound(0)
```

```
Console.WriteLine("Parameter name: " & _
                   methodParams(index).Name)
Console.WriteLine("Parameter position: " & _
                   methodParams(index).Position)
Console.WriteLine("Parameter type: {0}", _
                   methodParams(index).ParameterType)
Console.WriteLine("Optional?: " & _
                   methodParams(index).IsOptional)
Next
```

The output from this code is:

```
Parameter name: number
Parameter position: 0
Parameter type: System.Double
Optional?: False
```

MANIPULATING CLASS OBJECTS USING REFLECTION

The techniques we used in the previous section to examine the metadata of a class can also be used to manipulate the methods of a class. Using methods in this way is known as dynamic invocation, since we are creating the class objects at runtime and not at compile-time.

Using dynamic invocation, we can call class constructors, set and/or change class data members (even Private members), invoke Property methods, and invoke class methods (even Private methods). Many of these techniques, especially involving Private class members, should be used with caution, since data and methods are declared Private for good reasons. Nevertheless, there are times when accessing Private members using reflection is necessary and worth the risk it involves.

Invoking a Class Constructor

The first step in dynamically invoking a class is to create a class instance. Class instances are created via the class constructor. Let's start by looking at how to dynamically instantiate a NumberRange object.

Since we are creating our class object dynamically, we don't declare a NumberRange object. Instead, we use a generic object that will take on the characteristics of a NumberRange object after we dynamically invoke the constructor. We also need to create a Type object instantiated with the Get-Type method called with the NumberRange class as the argument. Here's the code:

```
Dim classType As Type = GetType(NumberRange)
Dim classObject As Object
```

To invoke the constructor, we use the GetConstructors() method to return the constructors for the NumberRange class:

```
Dim classCons() As ConstructorInfo =
  classType.GetConstructors(BindingFlags.Instance Or _
                            BindingFlags.Public Or _
                            BindingFlags.NonPublic)
Dim constr As ConstructorInfo
constr = classCons(0)
```

You have to pass at least the combination of BindingFlags attributes given in this parameter list. The method returns all the constructors defined for the class. However, we're only interested in the parameterized constructor, which is stored in the first position in the array.

To invoke this particular constructor, we declare a ConstructorInfo object and assign the first constructor stored in the array to that object. Now we're ready to invoke the constructor to instantiate a NumberRange object:

```
Dim params() As Object = {0, 100}
classObj = constr.Invoke(params)
```

The Invoke method can take several forms since it is overloaded. In this case, we only provide one argument—a list of parameters to pass to the constructor. The parameter list has to be passed as an Object, which is why the params array in the first line is declared as such. The Invoke method that is called on a ConstructorInfo object causes the underlying class's constructor to be called with the parameters stored in the params array, returning an instance of the underlying class.

Invoking a Class Method

One of the most common things you will do when using reflection with a class is to dynamically invoke a class method. We can use the Invoke method for class methods as well as for class constructors. Let's pass a number to the InRange method to see if it is within the range specified in the constructor.

The first step we have to take is to create a MethodInfo object. We can do this with the GetMethod method:

```
Dim theMethod As MethodInfo = classObj.GetType(). _
                          GetMethod("InRange")
```

The theMethod object now refers to the NumberRange method InRange.

All we have to do now is invoke the method using the Invoke method. In this particular use of the method, we have to pass both our class object and the method's parameters as arguments. The parameters' argument, as before, has to be passed as an Object array, even though in this case we only have a single parameter to pass to the method. Here's the code fragment, along with some code to test the return value from the method invocation:

```
Dim within As Boolean
Dim number() As Object = {65}
within = theMethod.Invoke(classObj, number)
If (within) Then
  Console.WriteLine(number(0) & " is within range.")
Else
  Console.WriteLine(number(0) & " is out of range.")
End If
```

Another way to invoke a class method is to use the InvokeMember method. This method differs from the Invoke method primarily by the fact that it is called directly from the dynamically created class object rather than from one of the Info classes (ConstructorInfo, PropertyInfo, MethodInfo, etc.).

The InvokeMember method takes five arguments:

- name (String)—the name of the method to invoke;
- invokeAttr (BindingFlags)—a set of one or more binding flags that tell the method how to search for the specified member and how to treat the member;

- binder (Binder)—an argument used primarily to make conversions from given argument types to formal argument types;
- target (Object)—the instance of the type whose member is being invoked; and
- params() (Object)—a list of the parameters to be passed to the member method.

Now let's see how to use this method. We'll create another number to test as we did previously, but this time, we invoke the InRange method using the InvokeMember method instead of the Invoke method. Here's the code:

```
Dim newNumber() As Object = {125}
within = classObj.GetType(). _
        InvokeMember("InRange", BindingFlags. _
                InvokeMethod, Nothing, _
                classObj, newNumber)
If (within) Then
  Console.WriteLine(number(0) & " is within range.")
Else
  Console.WriteLine(newNumber(0) & " is out of range.")
End If
```

The primary reason you will want to use the InvokeMember method over the Invoke method is flexibility. The InvokeMember method will automatically convert argument types into the proper type and it will also automatically search overloaded methods to find the right method to call based on the type and number of parameters passed in the method call. The Invoke method does not provide all of this support.

Dynamically Setting and Getting Property Values

We've seen how to return the properties of a class using reflection; we can also use reflection to set the properties of a class object (dynamically created, of course). There are two methods of the PropertyInfo class we can use for these purposes—SetValue and GetValue—and we can also use the InvokeMember method we discussed earlier.

The most straightforward way to modify property values using reflection is to call the SetValue and GetValue methods. These methods are found in the PropertyInfo class. The GetValue method takes two arguments—1. the property you want to retrieve and 2. a binding attribute that describes how to find the property. The binding attribute needs to include the flags Public, GetProperty, and Instance to work with a Public property.

The following code fragment returns the minimum value in the numeric range of the examples we've been working with in this chapter:

```
Dim lowProp As PropertyInfo
lowProp = classObj.GetType.GetProperty _
            ("Low", BindingFlags.Public Or _
            BindingFlags.GetProperty Or _
            BindingFlags.Instance)
Console.WriteLine("The minimum value in the range is " _
            & lowProp.GetValue(classObj, _
            Nothing). ToString)
```

To set a property, you call the SetValue method with three arguments: an instance of the method whose property you are setting, the new property value as an Object, and an indexer if the property is indexed. If the property is nonindexed, a Nothing (null) value should be used.

The following code fragment sets the new minimum value of the numeric range to 20 and then returns the property again to confirm that the set worked:

```
Dim lowVal As Object
lowVal = 20
lowProp.SetValue(classObj, lowVal, Nothing)
Console.WriteLine("The minimum value in the range is " _
            & lowProp.GetValue(classObj, _
            Nothing). ToString)
```

As we mentioned earlier, we can also set and retrieve properties using the InvokeMember method. Using this method with property values is similar to using it with class methods. The first argument is the property name; the second argument is the binding flags attribute combination, the third argument is a Binder object (usually Nothing), the fourth argument is an instantiated class object, and the fifth argument is an array consisting of the parameters to the Property method.

In the following example, we use the InvokeMember method to return the highest value in the numeric range:

```
Dim highVal As Double
highVal = CDbl(classType.InvokeMember _
                  ("High", BindingFlags.Public Or _
                  BindingFlags.GetProperty Or _
                  BindingFlags.Instance, Nothing, _
                  classObj, Nothing))
Console.WriteLine("The maximum value in the range is " _
                  & highVal)
```

The next code fragment changes the high value of the range by accessing the High property of the class:

```
Dim HighValues() As Object = {90}
classType.InvokeMember("High", BindingFlags.Public Or _
                      BindingFlags.SetProperty Or _
                      BindingFlags.Instance, Nothing, _
                      classObj, HighValues)
highVal = CDbl(classType.InvokeMember _
                  ("High", BindingFlags.Public Or _
                  BindingFlags.GetProperty Or _
                  BindingFlags.Instance, Nothing, _
                  classObj, Nothing))
Console.WriteLine("The maximum value in the range is " _
                  & highVal)
```

Dynamically Manipulating Data Member Values

Data member (field) values can be accessed dynamically using methods in the FieldInfo class as well as by the InvokeMember method. We'll start with the GetValue and SetValue methods of the FieldInfo class.

To use these two methods, you must first create a FieldInfo object that includes a reference to the data member you are trying to access. A FieldInfo object is created by calling the GetField method with the following arguments: the data member name and a binding flags combination attribute.

The GetValue method is called from the FieldInfo object you just created. The method takes just one argument, the class object used as a reference when creating the FieldInfo object.

The following code accesses the lowValue data member of our dynamically invoked class:

```
Dim lowField As FieldInfo = classObj.GetType.GetField _
                            ("lowValue", _
                            BindingFlags.NonPublic Or _
                            BindingFlags.Instance)
Console.WriteLine("lowValue: " & lowField.GetValue _
            (classObj).ToString)
```

To change a data member's value, we use the SetValue method. This method takes two arguments: the class object and the new value for the data member. The following code fragment changes the lowValue to a new value and then accesses it to ensure the change has been made properly:

```
lowField.SetValue(classObj, 30)
lowField = classObj.GetType.GetField("lowValue", _
                            BindingFlags.NonPublic Or _
                            BindingFlags.Instance)
Console.WriteLine("lowValue: " & lowField.GetValue _
            (classObj).ToString)
```

A word of caution is in order here. As we've advocated throughout this book, you should always try to modify Private data member values via Property methods only. This is always considered to be the best practice when performing "standard" OOP. However, reflection is not normally used in situations when standard OOP is performed. For example, when reflection is used for a special purpose, such as a debugging tool, and modifying a data member value via a Property method will lead to inefficient code, you will probably want to modify the value using the techniques learned here. Just remember, though, that the protections you've built into your Property methods will not be available, and subtle, or even not-so-subtle, bugs can result.

You can also modify (and view) data member values using the Invoke-Member method. The method is called with the following arguments: the data member name, a binding flag attribute combination, a Binder object, the class object as the target, and either a value if you are setting a data member value or Nothing if you are retrieving a data member value.

Here's a code fragment that accesses the highValue data member:

```
Dim highVals() As Object = {95}
classObj.GetType.InvokeMember("highValue", _
                              BindingFlags.Public Or _
                              BindingFlags.SetField Or _
                              BindingFlags.NonPublic Or _
                              BindingFlags.Instance, _
                              Nothing, classObj, highVals)
Dim hValue As Double
hValue = CDbl(classObj.GetType.InvokeMember _
              ("highValue", BindingFlags.Public Or _
              BindingFlags.GetField Or _
              BindingFlags.NonPublic Or _
              BindingFlags.Instance, Nothing, _
              classObj, Nothing))
Console.WriteLine("high value: " & hValue)
```

Either technique (FieldInfo class or InvokeMember) can be used to access data member values. Be sure, though, that with whatever technique you choose you are careful not to introduce bad data into your dynamic class object.

Let's wrap up this section by listing the complete program we've been working with:

```
Imports System.Reflection

Module Module1
  Public Class NumberRange

    Private lowValue As Double
    Private highValue As Double

    Public Sub New(ByVal low As Integer, ByVal high As Integer)
      lowValue = low
      highValue = high
    End Sub

    Public Sub New()
      lowValue = 0
      highValue = 0
    End Sub
```

```vbnet
  Public Property Low() As Double
    Get
      Return lowValue
    End Get
    Set(ByVal Value As Double)
      lowValue = Value
    End Set
  End Property
  Public Property High() As Double
    Get
      Return highValue
    End Get
    Set(ByVal Value As Double)
      highValue = Value
    End Set
  End Property
  Public Function InRange(ByVal number As Double) As Boolean
    If (number >= lowValue And number <= highValue) Then
      Return True
    Else
      Return False
    End If
  End Function
End Class
Sub Main()
  ' Create some objects to dynamically control
  Dim classType As Type = GetType(NumberRange)
  Dim classObj As Object
  Dim classCons() As ConstructorInfo = _
   classType.GetConstructors(BindingFlags.Instance Or _
   BindingFlags.Public Or BindingFlags.NonPublic)
  ' Invoke class constructor dynamically
  Dim constr As ConstructorInfo
  constr = classCons(0)
  Dim params() As Object = {0, 100}
  classObj = constr.Invoke(params)
  ' Invoke InRange method dynamically and test result
  Dim within As Boolean
  Dim number() As Object = {65}
  Dim theMethod As MethodInfo = _
   classObj.GetType().GetMethod("InRange")
  within = theMethod.Invoke(classObj, number)
```

```
If (within) Then
   Console.WriteLine(number(0) & " is within range.")
Else
   Console.WriteLine(number(0) & " is out of range.")
End If
' Dynamically call Property methods
Dim lowProp As PropertyInfo
Dim lowVal As Object
lowVal = 20
lowProp = classObj.GetType.GetProperty_
          ("Low", BindingFlags.Public _
          Or BindingFlags.GetProperty _
          Or BindingFlags.Instance)
lowProp.SetValue(classObj, lowVal, Nothing)
Console.WriteLine("The minimum value in the range is " & _
                  lowProp.GetValue(classObj, Nothing). _
                  ToString)
Dim highVal As Double
highVal = CDbl(classType.InvokeMember _
                  ("High", BindingFlags.Public Or _
                  BindingFlags.GetProperty Or _
                  BindingFlags.Instance, Nothing, _
                  classObj, Nothing))
Console.WriteLine("The maximum value in the range is " & _
                  highVal)
Dim HighValues() As Object = {90}
classType.InvokeMember("High", BindingFlags.Public Or _
                       BindingFlags.SetProperty Or _
                       BindingFlags.Instance, Nothing, _
                       classObj, HighValues)
highVal = CDbl(classType.InvokeMember ("High", _
               BindingFlags.Public Or _
               BindingFlags.GetProperty Or _
               BindingFlags.Instance, Nothing, _
               classObj, Nothing))
Console.WriteLine("The maximum value in the range is " & _
                  highVal)
' Accessing and modifying data member values with FieldInfo
Dim lowField As FieldInfo = classObj.GetType.GetField _
                              ("lowValue", _
                              BindingFlags.NonPublic Or _
                              BindingFlags.Instance)
```

```
      Console.WriteLine("lowValue: " & lowField.GetValue _
                        (classObj).ToString)
      lowField.SetValue(classObj, 30)
      lowField = classObj.GetType.GetField _
                ("lowValue", BindingFlags.NonPublic Or _
                 BindingFlags.Instance)
      Console.WriteLine("lowValue: " & lowField.GetValue _
                        (classObj).ToString)

      ' Accessing and modifying data member values with
      ' InvokeMember
      Dim highVals() As Object = {95}
      classObj.GetType.InvokeMember("highValue", _
                                    BindingFlags.Public Or _
                                    BindingFlags.SetField Or _
                                    BindingFlags.NonPublic Or _
                                    BindingFlags.Instance, _
                                    Nothing, classObj, highVals)
      Dim hValue As Double
      hValue = CDbl(classObj.GetType.InvokeMember _
               ("highValue", BindingFlags.Public Or _
               BindingFlags.GetField Or _
               BindingFlags.NonPublic Or _
               BindingFlags.Instance, Nothing, _
               classObj, Nothing))
      Console.WriteLine("high value: " & hValue)
      Console.Read()
   End Sub

End Module
```

ATTRIBUTES AND REFLECTION

Attributes are objects that are associated with particular elements of a VB.NET program. Using attributes, a programmer can insert custom metadata for a program. These metadata can be used to control class objects, serialize class data (see the next chapter), and even control how a VB.NET program is compiled (conditional compilation).

What Are Attributes?

An attribute is an object that a programmer can attach to the element of a program that provides extra information (or metadata) about the element.

There are two types of attributes—custom and intrinsic. An intrinsic attribute is an attribute added by the VB.NET system when you create a program. A custom attribute is an attribute the programmer adds to a program.

When an attribute is added to a program, the compiler inserts an attribute object in the MSIL code generated by the compiler. When the Common Language Runtime (CLR) comes across an attribute object, it performs the service defined by the attribute. Attributes, because they are objects, inherit from the System.Attribute class. This allows us to create custom attributes, along with using the intrinsic attributes inherent in VB.NET code.

INTRINSIC ATTRIBUTES

An intrinsic attribute is an attribute that is automatically applied to a VB.NET program, as opposed to a custom attribute, which is created and applied by a programmer. Intrinsic attributes don't automatically appear in code, though. The programmer must still add the attribute to the code for the compiler to recognize it, but the attribute itself is predefined by VB.NET.

The next chapter on object serialization discusses one use of attributes in depth. In this section, we'll examine a less complex attribute that allows you to perform conditional compilation.

Custom Attributes

We are not limited to the built-in attributes that are part of the VB.NET System. We can also create custom attributes that behave just like the intrinsic type.

One use of custom attributes might be to keep track of changes to a class definition. Of course, you could just use comments, such as

```
' Fields added on 2/25/2003 by Mike McMillan
```

but comments are hard to work with if, say, you want to add the comments to a database. In fact, there is no simple way to programmatically parse a comment to store its parts in a database. Also, comments are by nature unstructured, which makes parsing them problematic.

Attributes, in contrast, are both structured and easy to work with programmatically using reflection. A comment can be replaced by an attribute such as this one:

```
<ProgramUpdate(1, "Added fields", "2/13/2003", _
              "McMillan")> _
```

The attributes that are added to the class definition can then be retrieved, parsed, and added to a database using reflection. In this situation, attributes provide utility that comments can never provide.

The first step in creating a custom attribute is to declare the class and inherit the Attribute class. The class heading for the ProgramUpdate class looks like this:

```
Public Class ProgramUpdate
   Inherits System.Attribute
```

The next step is to declare the custom attribute. This is performed using, of all things, an attribute. The declaration informs the compiler which class elements can be used with the attribute target. A typical attribute declaration looks like this:

```
<AttributeUsage(AttributeTargets.Class Or _
                AttributeTargets.Method Or _
                AttributeTargets.Constructor Or _
                AttributeTargets.Property Or _
                AttributeTargets.Field, _
                AllowMultiple:=True)> _
```

In a sense, this declaration actually involves meta-metadata, since it deals with data about the type of attribute we are about to create. The declaration says that our attribute can be used on the following targets: classes, methods, constructors, properties, and fields (data members). The second argument says that we can declare multiple attributes on any of the elements in the first argument. This declaration actually goes before the class heading, though we've introduced it after the class heading here.

Like any other class, an Attribute class has data members for storing the data passed in when an attribute is written. The data members for the ProgramUpdate class are

```
Private UpdateNumber As Integer
Private UpdateDescription As String
Private UpdateDate As String
Private UpdateWho As String
```

An attribute class must have a constructor method, typically a fully param-eterized method. There's really no reason to have a default constructor since our only use of an attribute object is to provide all the parts of the attribute when the attribute is used.

An attribute class constructor can take two types of parameters—positional and named. For now, we'll discuss positional parameters, which are more typical. We'll take a look at named parameters at the end of this section.

The following code defines the constructor method for the ProgramUpdate class:

```
Public Sub New(ByVal number As Integer, _
               ByVal desc As String, _
               ByVal upDate As String, _
               ByVal who As String)
   UpdateNumber = number
   UpdateDescription = desc
   UpdateDate = upDate
   UpdateWho = who
End Sub
```

Next, we declare some Property methods for returning the data stored in a ProgramUpdate object:

```
ReadOnly Property Number() As Integer
   Get
      Return UpdateNumber
   End Get
End Property

ReadOnly Property Description() As String
   Get
      Return UpdateDescription
   End Get
End Property

ReadOnly Property TheDate() As String
   Get
      Return UpdateDate
   End Get
End Property
```

```
ReadOnly Property Who() As String
  Get
    Return UpdateWho
  End Get
End Property
```

Each Property method is declared ReadOnly because we only want to be able to retrieve each element of a ProgramUpdate object; we don't want the user to be able to set any of the elements outside of the constructor.

That's all we need for an Attribute class. Let's look at a class definition with a single attribute added to the definition, along with a test program that returns information about the attribute:

```
<ProgramUpdate(1, "Added fields", "2/25/2003", _
               "McMillan")> _
Public Class NumberRange

  Private lowValue As Double
  Private highValue As Double

  Public Sub New(ByVal low As Integer, ByVal high As _
                 Integer)
    lowValue = low
    highValue = high
  End Sub

  Public Sub New()
    lowValue = 0
    highValue = 0
  End Sub

  Public Property Low() As Double
    Get
      Return lowValue
    End Get

    Set(ByVal Value As Double)
      lowValue = Value
    End Set
  End Property
```

```
    Public Property High() As Double
      Get
        Return highValue
      End Get
      Set(ByVal Value As Double)
        highValue = Value
      End Set
    End Property

    Public Function InRange(ByVal number As Double) As _
                           Boolean
      If (number >= lowValue And number <= highValue) Then
        Return True
      Else
        Return False
      End If
    End Function

End Class

Sub Main()
  Dim grades As New NumberRange(0, 100)
  Dim metaGrade As MemberInfo = GetType(NumberRange)
  Dim attributes() As Object
  attributes = metaGrade.GetCustomAttributes(False)
  Dim attrib As Object
  For Each attrib In attributes
    Console.WriteLine("Number: " & _
                      CType(attrib, ProgramUpdate).Number)
    Console.WriteLine("Description: " & CType(attrib, _
                      ProgramUpdate).Description)
    Console.WriteLine("Date: " & CType(attrib, _
                      ProgramUpdate).TheDate)
    Console.WriteLine("Who: " & CType(attrib, _
                      ProgramUpdate).Who)
  Next
  Console.Write("Finished.")
  Console.Read()
End Sub
```

Multiple attributes can be added to a class definition. All you have to do is separate each attribute with a comma, like this:

```
<ProgramUpdate(1, "Added fields", "2/25/2003", "McMillan")> _
ProgramUpdate(2, "Added constructor", "2/26/2003", "Durr"), _
ProgramUpdate(3, "Added properties", "2/26/2003", "Williams")> _

Public Class NumberRange

Private lowValue As Double
Private highValue As Double
  . . .
```

To wrap up our discussion of custom attributes, let's look at how to use named parameters in an Attribute class constructor. We can pick any parameter to be the named parameter, but to make modification easy, we'll pick the last data member, UpdateWho.

To make this a named parameter we have to do two things: 1. take the data member out of the parameter list of the constructor method and 2. make the Who property a read/write property instead of read-only. Here are the two pertinent code fragments from the ProgramUpdate definition:

```
Public Sub New(ByVal number As Integer, _
               ByVal desc As String, _
               ByVal upDate As String)
   UpdateNumber = number
   UpdateDescription = desc
   UpdateDate = upDate
End Sub
. . .
Public Property Who() As String
   Get
      Return UpdateWho
   End Get
   Set(ByVal value As String)
      UpdateWho = value
   End Set
End Property
```

The attribute is added to the program like this:

```
<ProgramUpdate(1, "Added fields", "2/25/2003", _
              Who:="McMillan")> _

Public Class NumberRange
. . .
```

SUMMARY

Reflection refers to VB.NET's ability to examine the inner workings of classes (and programs). You can use reflection to discover the data types declared in a class, the methods defined in the class, and any other defined feature of a class definition. Besides just discovering this information, called metadata, you can also use reflection to invoke a method, making the class method behave much like a standard subprogram.

Attributes allow you to create your own metadata. Attributes can be used for many tasks, including creating "smart" comments and object serialization. There are many predefined attributes in VB.NET, including the serialization attributes. You can also create your own attribute classes for custom attributes.

EXERCISES

1. In an earlier chapter you developed a Name class. Using reflection, write a program that reports all the data members, constructors, and methods (including Property methods) in the class. Before you begin this exercise, read Exercise 2, which you will perform at the same time as this one.
2. Use attributes to make comments of your work as you complete Exercise 1. Write a program that reads each attribute and writes all the comments to the console.

CHAPTER 11

Object Persistence: Serialization

Serialization is the process of capturing the current state of a class object and writing the state to disk. Serialization allows you to make a class object persistent, which means that you can save the current state of an object while a program is running and at a later time retrieve that state and continue using the object. In this chapter, we'll show you how to perform both serialization and deserialization, which is retrieving an object's state from disk.

SERIALIZATION DEFINED

Serialization in VB.NET involves writing out the state of a class object as a series of bytes to a byte stream. The CLR writes out a class object as an object-graph, which consists of the class object and all the member data associated with the object. To let the CLR know that a class can be serialized, it must be marked with the Serializable attribute.

Although classes must be marked to be serialized, primitive types do not have to be marked as such. Therefore, all the primitive types within your class definition will be serialized automatically when the class is marked Serializable. Other objects (such as nested classes) within a class definition must be tagged with the Serializable attribute if they are to be serialized with the rest of the class types.

A class is physically serialized using a formatter. A formatter, as its name suggests, defines the format of the data stream that is written to disk. The two most common formats for serializing VB.NET objects are binary format and SOAP (Simple Object Access Protocol) format.

Most programmers are familiar with binary format, but many are as yet unfamiliar with SOAP. SOAP, a protocol based on XML (Extensible Markup Language), was designed for the exchange of information on the Web. Because it is designed for transmission over the Internet, it is a fairly simple, lightweight, modular, and extensible protocol.

The general rule to adhere to in choosing the right format is as follows: If you are designing your serialized objects for local or network access, use the binary format; if you are designing your serialized objects for Internet access, use SOAP format. Because we don't have the space to fully discuss XML here, however, we limit our discussion to serialization to the binary format.

SERIALIZING A CLASS OBJECT

There are just a few steps necessary to serialize a class object. The first step is to import the necessary namespaces to perform serialization. We'll need two namespaces:

- System.Runtime.Serialization and
- System.Runtime.Serialization.Formatters.Binary.

The next step is to mark the class as serializable. This is accomplished using the Serializable attribute. The following code demonstrates how a class is made serializable:

```
Imports System.Runtime.Serialization
Imports System.Runtime.Serialization.Formatters.Binary

Module Module1

  <Serializable()> _
```

```
Public Class Name

  Private first As String
  Private middle As String
  Private last As String

  . . .
```

Within the class, those types that you don't want to serialize can be marked with the Nonserialized attribute. We'll look at how to do this later.

Next we need to create a method in our class for serializing the object. The method code will first instantiate a file stream object and a formatter object. When the file stream object is instantiated, the call to the constructor names the physical file to hold the data stream and calls the proper mode of the file stream object (Create). The method then calls the Serialize method of the formatter object to serialize the class object.

Next we need the code for the Serialize method. Also, you need to import the System.IO namespace to use the FileStream class. Here's the code for the Serialize method:

```
Public Sub Serialize()
  Dim fileStream As New FileStream("c:\nameout.ser", _
                                 FileMode.Create)
  Dim binFormat As New BinaryFormatter()
  binFormat.Serialize(fileStream, Me)
  fileStream.Close()
End Sub
```

Notice that the fileStream object is closed before the method finishes. While this is mainly just good programming practice, it also ensures that we can access the file to deserialize the object in the same program invocation if we choose.

Now let's look at some code that actually serializes a Name object:

```
Sub Main()
  Dim myName As New Name("Michael", "M", "McMillan")
  myName.Serialize()
  Console.Write("Finished. . .")
  Console.Read()
End Sub
```

Figure 11.1 shows the nameout.ser file where the serialized object is stored.

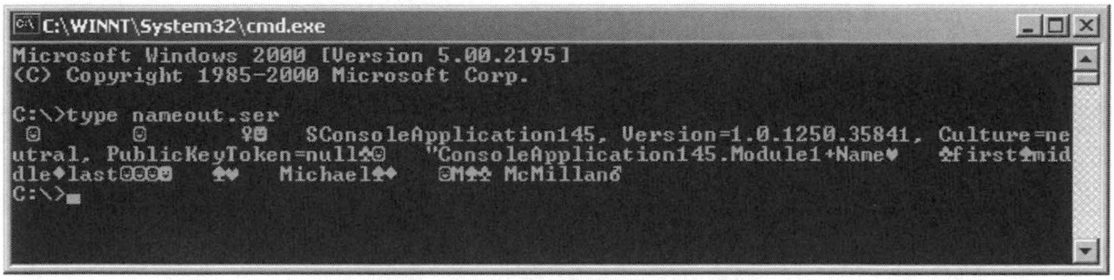

FIGURE 11.1. The nameout.ser File

The information saved in the serialized file includes the name of the application, the version of VB.NET, the names of the Private data members, and the data stored in them when the object was serialized.

Serializing an object is easy enough. This particular example used the binary formatter, though we could have chosen to use the SOAP formatter. Before we look at how to do that, let's look at how we can deserialize this class object and load it into a new VB.NET program.

DESERIALIZING A CLASS OBJECT

Deserializing a class object is just as straightforward as serializing. The Formatter.Binary class has a method used for deserializing an object—Deserialize. This method returns the class object serialized to disk, so you need a class object to receive the return value when the method is called.

To call the Deserialize method, we need a file stream object to open the file stream stored to disk, and we need a binary formatter object to call the method. The following code shows a new method added to the Name class that deserializes a class object:

```
Shared Function Deserialize(ByVal serialFile _
                            As String) As Name
    Dim fileStream As New FileStream(serialFile, _
                                     FileMode.Open)
    Dim binFormat As New BinaryFormatter()
    Return binFormat.Deserialize(fileStream)
End Function
```

The method is declared Shared because we want to be able to call the method without a specific Name instance, since we are using the method to create a specific instance of the class.

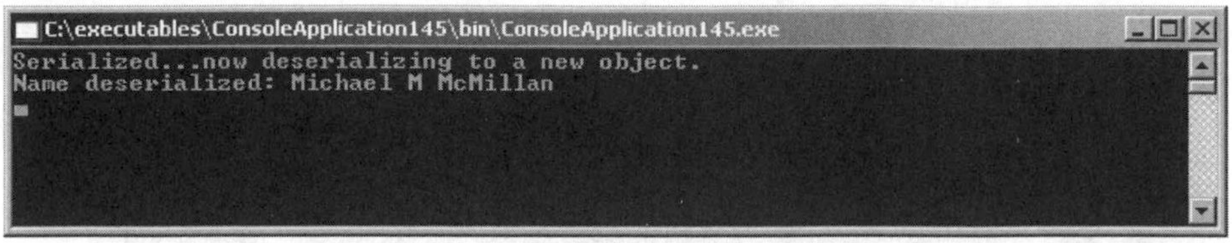

FIGURE **11.2.** Output from Code Fragment

Now let's look at a code fragment that uses the Deserialize method:

```
Dim sFile As String = "c:\nameout.ser"
Dim newName As Name = CType(Name.Deserialize(sFile), _
                 Name)
Console.WriteLine("Name deserialized: " & _
            newName.ToString())
```

The output from this code fragment, along with the output from earlier, is shown in Figure 11.2.

Here is the complete program, along with the class definition, that serializes and deserializes a Name object:

```
Imports System.Runtime.Serialization
Imports System.Runtime.Serialization.Formatters.Binary
Imports System.IO

Module Module1
<Serializable()> _
Public Class Name

  Private first As String
  Private middle As String
  Private last As String

  Public Sub New(ByVal first As String, ByVal middle _
           As String, ByVal last As String)
    Me.first = first
    Me.middle = middle
    Me.last = last
  End Sub

  Public Function GetFirst() As String
    Return Me.first
  End Function
```

```
   Public Function GetMiddle() As String
      Return Me.middle
   End Function

   Public Function GetLast() As String
      Return Me.last
   End Function

   Public Sub SetFirst(ByVal first As String)
      Me.first = first
   End Sub

   Public Sub SetMiddle(ByVal middle As String)
      Me.middle = middle
   End Sub

   Public Sub SetLast(ByVal last As String)
      Me.last = last
   End Sub

   Public Overrides Function ToString() As String
      Return Me.first & " " & Me.middle & " " & Me.last
   End Function

   Public Sub Serialize()
      Dim fileStream As New FileStream("c:\nameout.ser", _
                                  FileMode.Create)
      Dim binFormat As New BinaryFormatter()
      binFormat.Serialize(fileStream, Me)
      fileStream.Close()
   End Sub

   Shared Function Deserialize(ByVal serialFile As _
                            String) As Name
      Dim fileStream As New FileStream(serialFile, _
                                  FileMode.Open)
      Dim binFormat As New BinaryFormatter()
      Return binFormat.Deserialize(fileStream)
   End Function

End Class

Sub Main()
   Dim myName As New Name("Michael", "M", "McMillan")
   myName.Serialize()
```

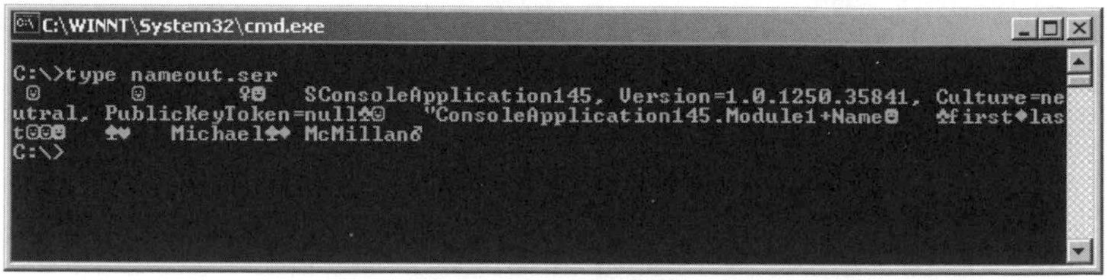

FIGURE **11.3. Output from the Complete Program**

```
    Console.WriteLine("Serialized . . . now
deserializing _
                    to a new object.")
    Dim sFile As String = "c:\nameout.ser"
    Dim newName As Name = _
     CType(Name.Deserialize(sFile), Name)
    Console.WriteLine("Name deserialized: " & _
                    newName.ToString())
    Console.Read()
  End Sub

End Module
```

LEAVING DATA UNSERIALIZED

As we mentioned earlier, you don't have to serialize all the data stored in a class object. Data you want to leave unserialized can be marked with the Nonserialized attribute. All other data in the class will be serialized except the data marked Nonserialized.

Let's use the Name class again. In this example we elect not to serialize middle name data in a class object to disk when a class object is serialized. Only the first lines of the class code are shown, since nothing else after the Nonserialized attribute has changed:

```
Imports System.Runtime.Serialization
Imports System.Runtime.Serialization.Formatters.Binary
Imports System.IO

Module Module1

  <Serializable()> _
```

```
Public Class Name

  Private first As String

  <NonSerialized()> _
  Private middle As String

  Private last As String
        . . .
```

The output from the complete program is shown in Figure 11.3. Notice that only the first name and the last name are serialized to disk. The middle name is excluded.

SUMMARY

Serializing a class is the process of capturing the current state of a class and writing that state to disk. Serializing is performed using attributes added to the code indicating you want the class to be serialized. Serialization is important if you want your classes and their states to persist from one invocation of a program to the next.

Deserializing a class restores a class to the state it was in when the class was serialized. This is performed using the Deserialize method.

EXERCISES

1. Create a TimeStamp class that stores the date and time. Write a program that creates a TimeStamp object, stores the current system time in the object, and serializes the object's data to disk. Write the program in Sub Main and do not write a class method for serialization.
2. Add a code segment to the program in Exercise 1 that deserializes the object, storing the data in a new TimeStamp object.
3. Modify the program in Exercise 1 so that the TimeStamp class includes methods for serialization and deserialization.

CHAPTER 12

Building a Windows Application

A Windows application is by necessity written in an object-oriented manner. This chapter discusses the code generated by VS.NET when a Windows application is built. We'll examine both the code generated by VS.NET and the code created when a programmer builds an application. We will also examine how to use object-oriented principles in the code the programmer adds to the application.

As the noted computer scientist and education theorist Seymour Paper once stated, "You can't think about thinking without thinking about thinking about something." Likewise, you can't examine building a Windows application without having a Windows application to build. To that end, the application we'll use to illustrate how object-oriented principles aid the creation of a Windows application is a basic calculator, similar to the one found in Windows. By picking a rather simple application that uses many widely employed Windows features (e.g., textboxes, buttons, and labels), we can focus on how taking an object-oriented approach makes the development easier and more efficient. We should also mention that this chapter is not designed to teach a novice how to create a Windows application; rather it teaches how to create a Windows application in an object-oriented way. We assume the reader already knows how to place controls on a form and already knows the basics of writing event-driven code.

VS.NET-GENERATED CODE

When you start a new Windows application project, VS.NET generates a skeleton of a program you'll use to build the application. The following code is an example of how a new Windows application looks from a code view:

```
Public Class Form1
    Inherits System.Windows.Forms.Form

#Region " Windows Form Designer generated code "

    Public Sub New()
      MyBase.New()
      ' This call is required by the Windows Form
      ' Designer.
      InitializeComponent()

      ' Add any initialization after the
      ' InitializeComponent() call

    End Sub

    ' Form overrides dispose to clean up the component
    ' list.

    Protected Overloads Overrides Sub Dispose _
      (ByVal disposing As Boolean)
      If disposing Then
        If Not (components Is Nothing) Then
          components.Dispose()
        End If
      End If
      MyBase.Dispose(disposing)
    End Sub

    ' Required by the Windows Form Designer
    Private components As System.ComponentModel.Container

    ' NOTE: The following procedure is required by
    ' the Windows Form
    ' Designer
    ' It can be modified using the Windows Form Designer.
    ' Do not modify it using the code editor.
```

```
<System.Diagnostics.DebuggerStepThrough()> _
 Private Sub InitializeComponent()
  '
  ' Form1
  '
  Me.AutoScaleBaseSize = _
   New System.Drawing.Size(5, 13)
  Me.ClientSize = New System.Drawing.Size(292, 273)
  Me.Name = "Form1"
  Me.Text = "Form1"
 End Sub

#End Region

End Class
```

This code should look somewhat familiar to you, even if you've never developed a Windows application before. A Windows application is encapsulated in a class named Form1. To place and use the different controls on the form, the class inherits from the System.Windows.Forms.Form class.

The next line marks the beginning of a Region, which is just a section of code whose view can be expanded or contracted (a tree view). The region contains all the code generated by VS.NET when we tell it we want to develop a Windows application.

The next section of code is the constructor method for the Form1 class. The method calls the constructor for the base class and then calls a private method, InitializeComponent. We'll look at the definition of this method later.

The next method, Dispose, is called when an application stops. It is similar to a destructor method in C++. It cleans up the components placed on the form and then calls the Dispose method of the base class.

The last method in the class is InitializeComponent. It sets the size of the form and two properties—the name and the caption. Once we add some controls to the form, the code in this method will expand significantly, so we'll return to this method later to see what VS.NET puts here as we build the application.

CONSIDERING A CALCULATOR DESIGN

We begin developing our calculator program by considering how to design the application. The first step is to look at how a real calculator works. The

Windows calculator is a good model for us since we want to mimic its functionality in our program.

A CALCULATOR MODEL

There are several ways to implement a calculator program. Most serious implementations parse the arithmetic expression and store each token in some type of data structures. The two data structures that are used most often are the binary tree and the stack. The calculator in this chapter uses two stacks to store the operands and the operators punched into the calculator.

The Stack Data Structure

The stack is one of the oldest and most commonly used data structures in computer science. A stack allows just three primary operations: Push, Pop, and Peek. Data are stored in a stack by "pushing" the data onto the stack. A data item that has just been pushed onto the stack is stored at the "top" of the stack. When another item is stored on the stack, the item at the top gets pushed down and the new item is then stored at the top.

The only way to remove data from a stack is to pop the data off the stack. The only data item that can be popped off the stack is the item at the top of the stack. If there is more than one item stored on the stack, after an item is popped off the stack, the next item down is moved up to the top of the stack.

An everyday analogy to the stack data structure is the stack of trays at a cafeteria. You can only get a tray by grabbing the top tray on the stack, and you can only place a new tray on the top of the stack. Stacks are commonly used in programming languages to store variables and their values. You might be aware of this fact if you've ever written an "infinite" loop that eventually causes your computer system to halt, displaying an error message such as "Stack overflow."

Visual Basic.NET provides a Stack data structure in the Collections namespace. To use a stack, first import the Collections namespace (unless you're using VS.NET, which automatically imports the Collections namespace for you). Data are placed on a stack with the Push method. Data are removed from the stack with the Pop method. When data get popped from a stack, they are permanently removed from the stack. If you want to just examine the top value of a stack, use the Peek method, which returns the value at the top without removing it. There is also a Count property for determining the number of items in a stack. Our program also uses another useful method, Clear, which clears the contents of a stack.

The following short program demonstrates how to store data in a stack and then retrieve it. This particular program tests words to see if they are palindromes. Recall that a palindrome is a word or phrase that has the same spelling forward and backward. A short palindrome is "bob"; a long palindrome is "amana plan a canal panama."

A stack can be used to test for palindromes because a word we store in a stack will be removed from the stack in reverse. In other words, if we store the name "terri" in a stack, the last letter in ("i") will be the first letter out, giving us "irret" (which is not a palindrome, by the way).

Here's the program (in which the word to check is assigned directly to a variable):

```
Imports System.Collections
Module Module1
  Sub Main()
    Dim wordStack As New Stack()
    Dim word As String = "amanaplanacanalpanama"
    Dim index As Integer = 0
    For index = 0 To word.Length - 1
      wordStack.Push(word.Substring(index, 1))
    Next
    If (isPalindrome(wordStack, word)) Then
      Console.WriteLine(word & " is a palindrome.")
    Else
      Console.WriteLine(word & " is not a _
                    palindrome.")
    End If
    Console.Read()
  End Sub
  Function isPalindrome(ByVal st As Stack, ByVal w As _
                    String)
    Dim tempWord As String = ""
    Dim index = 0
    For index = 1 To st.Count
      tempWord &= st.Pop()
    Next
```

```
      If (tempWord = w) Then
        Return True
      Else
        Return False
      End If
    End Function
  End Module
```

Using a Stack in a Calculator Program

Our calculator program will use two stacks, one for the numbers and one for the operators. If we had to worry about operator precedence, then having the two stacks makes expression evaluation much easier to perform. For a calculator such as this one, however, having two stacks may be overkill, but we'll keep them since we may want to expand on the program later and having two stacks makes our program more general.

Our program uses the stacks like this: First, the user enters a number and then presses one of the arithmetic operators. At this point the number gets pushed onto the numeric stack and the operator gets pushed onto the operator stack. When a second number is entered and another operator is pressed, the program checks to make sure there are two numbers on the stack and an operator. If so, then the first number is popped into a variable (operand2) and the second number is popped into another variable (operand1). The reason the second number (the one deeper in the stack) is placed in operand2 is because for some operations, such as subtraction and division, the position of the operands matters. For example, suppose the expression the user enters is "4/2"; if we place the numbers in the wrong operands we get a result of 0.5 instead of 2.

Since this is a book on OOP, we will of course implement the part of the program that does the calculation as a class. This Calculator class, though, is used primarily for its methods and not so much for the data it encapsulates, so we can think of this class more as an application programming interface.

A CALCULATOR API

A very productive way to think of using a class in a program is to think of the class as an application programming interface (API). Some readers may be familiar with the Windows API, which is a set of functions that programming languages can access to perform low-level Windows programming. Other languages also use APIs, so the concept is a common one for most experienced programmers.

When we design a class for use as an API we don't really change how we design the class. We still need a constructor method and we need other methods for capturing the particular behavior we are modeling. However, we may not use some aspects of class design, such as Property methods, as much as we do when we are using a class more as a data type.

One advantage to building our Calculator class with an API in mind is that we can build the class without worrying about how we're going to use the class in a program. Since the interface to the class will be through method calls, we can use the class in a Console application or a Windows application without making any changes at all to the class. In fact, we originally designed this class *as* a Console application and then ported it directly to a Windows application, with no loss of functionality.

When we design a class to function as an API, we are primarily concerned with the Public methods that make up the interface of the API. For a Calculator API, we want methods for adding, subtracting, multiplying, and dividing, at the least. We also want a method that clears out the result. So far the class definition seems quite straightforward.

As for data members, we need just a few—one to store the results of calculations, two members for the operands, and two Stack members. Let's look now at the code for a Calculator class:

```
Public Class Calculator

    Private result, op1, op2 As Double
    Private numStack As New Stack()
    Private opStack As New Stack()

    Public Sub New()
      result = 0
    End Sub

    Public Sub Input(ByVal obj As Object)
      If (IsNumeric(obj)) Then
        numStack.Push(obj)
        result = numStack.Peek
        If (numStack.Count = 2 And opStack.Count >= 1) _
        Then
```

```
      EvalExpression()
    End If
  ElseIf (obj = "+" Or obj = "-" Or obj = "*" Or _
          obj = "/" Or obj = "=") Then
    opStack.Push(obj)
  End If
End Sub

Private Sub EvalExpression()
  Dim op1, op2 As Double
  Dim operator As String
  op2 = CDbl(numStack.Pop())
  op1 = CDbl(numStack.Pop())
  operator = CStr(opStack.Pop())
  Select Case operator
    Case "+"
      result = op1 + op2
    Case "-"
      result = op1 - op2
    Case "*"
      result = op1 * op2
    Case "/"
      result = op1 / op2
  End Select
  numStack.Push(result)
End Sub

Public Function Show() As Double
  Return result
End Function

Public Sub Clear()
  result = 0
  numStack.Clear()
  opStack.Clear()
End Sub

End Class
```

Almost all of the work in this class is performed by two methods: Input and EvalExpression. The public interface for this class consists of three methods: Input, Clear, and Show. Clear simply clears the result member and the two stacks, and Show returns the value of the calculator instance at any particular time.

The Input method is the nerve center of the class. The method naturally accepts all the input from the user and routes it accordingly. First, the method determines if the input is a number or an operator. If the input is a number, the method pushes the number onto the number stack and then checks to see how many numbers are on the number stack. If there are two numbers on that stack, and there is an operator on the operator stack, it calls the EvalExpression method. If the input is an operator, the method pushes the operator onto the operator stack.

The EvalExpression method performs a straightforward task. First, it pops off two numbers and stores them in two operand variables. Then it pops off the operator and stores it in a variable. The method then uses a Select Case statement to decide which operation to perform. After the operation is performed, the result is pushed onto the number stack.

The last operation in EvalExpression is important because, without storing the result on the stack, a long expression (2 * 2 * 2 * 2 * 2 =) would not be calculated correctly, since an intermediate result would be found and the next number entered would start a new expression.

DESIGNING THE CALCULATOR USER INTERFACE

We all know what a calculator looks like, and most of us have used the Windows calculator, so designing the user interface for our Calculator program is easy. Let's take a look at our user interface in design view and we'll discuss its components (Figure 12.1).

Admittedly, this is a very basic user interface and the user is encouraged to improve upon its appearance as an exercise in GUI development. The primary means of entering data is via the number buttons on the calculator. At the top of the calculator is a textbox that can be used for user input, but its primary purpose is to display user input and the result of calculations. The Clear button sets the display back to 0. The Equals button can be used to display the result of a calculation, as in this series of buttons pushed by the user: 4 + 3 =. The number 7 is displayed in the textbox. Alternatively, you can enter another operation key (+, −, *, /) after entering two numbers and an operator, as in 4 + 3 +. This series also results in the value 7 displayed in the textbox. Pushing an operator button after entering two operands indicates the user wants to continue performing calculations.

FIGURE 12.1. Windows Calculator

WRITING THE CALCULATOR PROGRAM CODE

Because we've already written the Calculator class, much of the code for this program is already written. The code we have to write in the Form1 class deals primarily with handling the events in the user interface. Having a class that handles the "business logic" of our program makes the user interface much easier to code. As you'll see, each button's Click event only has a few lines of code. We'll start our discussion by looking at how numbers are entered into the calculator.

The Number Buttons

When the user enters a number, he or she clicks the number buttons until the entire number has been entered. A number can consist of one or more button clicks. Here is the code for the number 1:

```
Private Sub One_Click(ByVal sender As System.Object, _
                      ByVal e As Ssystem.EventArgs) _
                      Handles One.Click
    checkOpPressed()
    Display.Text &= "1"
End Sub
```

To indicate when an operator is being entered, the program has a global variable, opPressed, that is initially set to False. If an operator is pressed, this variable is set to True; the next number entered is a new number and the display is cleared before the number is actually displayed. Here's the code for checkOpPressed:

```
Private Sub checkOpPressed()
  If (opPressed = True) Then
    Display.Text = ""
    opPressed = False
  End If
End Sub
```

Getting back to the One_Click code, we see that after the code checks to see if an operator has been pushed, the number 1 is concatenated to whatever is on the display at that time. And that's all there is to entering numbers.

The Operator Buttons

The operator buttons contain the code that interacts with the Calculator class. The code for the addition button is as follows:

```
Private Sub Addition_Click(ByVal sender As _
                           System.Object, ByVal e As _
                           System.EventArgs) Handles _
                           Addition.Click
  calc.input(CDbl(Display.Text))
  calc.input("+")
  opPressed = True
  Display.Text = calc.Show()
End Sub
```

The first line of the method sends the number shown in the calculator display (converted to Double) to the Calculator object. Then the operator associated with the button (in this case, the plus sign) is sent to the Calculator object. The oppressed variable is set to True and the result calculated by the Calculator object (if any) is assigned to the Display textbox. If you remember what happens in the Calculator class, when an operator is pushed onto the Operator stack, and there's just one number on the Numbers stack, that number becomes the intermediate result.

And that's the entire program. Here is the complete code to the Windows application, along with the code for the Calculator class:

```
Public Class Form1
   Inherits System.Windows.Forms.Form
   Dim calc As Calculator
   Dim opPressed As Boolean
#Region " Windows Form Designer generated code "

   Public Sub New()
     MyBase.New()
      ' This call is required by the Windows Form Designer.
     InitializeComponent()

      ' Add any initialization after the InitializeComponent()
      ' call
   End Sub

#End Region

   Private Sub Form1_Load(ByVal sender As System.Object, _
                         ByVal e As System.EventArgs) Handles _
                         MyBase.Load
     calc = New Calculator()
     opPressed = False
   End Sub

   Private Sub One_Click(ByVal sender As System.Object, _
                         ByVal e As System.EventArgs) Handles _
                         One.Click
     checkOpPressed()
     Display.Text &= "1"
   End Sub

   Private Sub Point_Click(ByVal sender As System.Object, _
                         ByVal e As System.EventArgs) Handles _
                         Point.Click
     checkOpPressed()
     Display.Text &= "."
   End Sub

   Private Sub Clear_Click(ByVal sender As System.Object, _
                         ByVal e As System.EventArgs) Handles _
                         Clear.Click
```

```
      Display.Text = ""
      calc.Clear()
   End Sub

   Private Sub Zero_Click(ByVal sender As System.Object, _
                        ByVal e As System.EventArgs) Handles _
                        Zero.Click
      checkOpPressed()
      Display.Text &= "0"
   End Sub

   Private Sub Two_Click(ByVal sender As System.Object, _
                        ByVal e As System.EventArgs) Handles _
                        Two.Click
      checkOpPressed()
      Display.Text &= "2"   .
   End Sub

   Private Sub Three_Click(ByVal sender As System.Object, _
                        ByVal e As System.EventArgs) Handles _
                        Three.Click
      checkOpPressed()
      Display.Text &= "3"
   End Sub

   Private Sub Four_Click(ByVal sender As System.Object, _
                        ByVal e As System.EventArgs) Handles _
                        Four.Click
      checkOpPressed()
      Display.Text &= "4"
   End Sub

   Private Sub Five_Click(ByVal sender As System.Object, _
                        ByVal e As System.EventArgs) Handles _
                        Five.Click
      checkOpPressed()
      Display.Text &= "5"
   End Sub

   Private Sub Six_Click(ByVal sender As System.Object, _
                        ByVal e As System.EventArgs) Handles _
                        Six.Click
      checkOpPressed()
      Display.Text &= "6"
   End Sub
```

```
   Private Sub Seven_Click(ByVal sender As System.Object, _
                            ByVal e As System.EventArgs) Handles _
                            Seven.Click
      checkOpPressed()
      Display.Text &= "7"
   End Sub

   Private Sub Eight_Click(ByVal sender As System.Object, _
                            ByVal e As System.EventArgs) Handles _
                            Eight.Click
      checkOpPressed()
      Display.Text &= "8"
   End Sub

   Private Sub Nine_Click(ByVal sender As System.Object, _
                            ByVal e As System.EventArgs) Handles _
                            Nine.Click
      checkOpPressed()
      Display.Text &= "9"
   End Sub

   Private Sub Addition_Click(ByVal sender As System.Object, _
                            ByVal e As System.EventArgs) _
                            Handles Addition.Click
      calc.input(CDbl(Display.Text))
      calc.input("+")
      opPressed = True
      Display.Text = calc.Show()
   End Sub
   Private Sub checkOpPressed()
      If (opPressed = True) Then
        Display.Text = ""
        opPressed = False
      End If
   End Sub

   Private Sub Subtraction_Click(ByVal sender As System.Object, _
                            ByVal e As System.EventArgs) _
                            Handles Subtraction.Click
      calc.input(CDbl(Display.Text))
      calc.input("-")
      opPressed = True
      Display.Text = calc.Show()
   End Sub
```

```
Private Sub Multiply_Click(ByVal sender As System.Object, _
                        ByVal e As System.EventArgs) _
                        Handles Multiply.Click
   calc.input(CDbl(Display.Text))
   calc.input("*")
   opPressed = True
   Display.Text = calc.Show()
End Sub

Private Sub Divide_Click(ByVal sender As System.Object, _
                        ByVal e As System.EventArgs) Handles_
                        Divide.Click
   calc.input(CDbl(Display.Text))
   calc.input("/")
   opPressed = True
   Display.Text = calc.Show()
End Sub

Private Sub Equals_Click(ByVal sender As System.Object, _
                        ByVal e As System.EventArgs) _
                        Handles Equals.Click
   calc.input(CDbl(Display.Text))
   calc.input("=")
   opPressed = True
   Display.Text = calc.Show
End Sub
End Class
Public Class Calculator
   Private result, op1, op2 As Double
   Private numStack As New Stack()
   Private opStack As New Stack()
   Public Sub New()
     result = 0
   End Sub
   Public Sub input(ByVal obj As Object)
     If (IsNumeric(obj)) Then
       numStack.Push(obj)
       ' result = CDbl(obj)
       result = numStack.Peek
       If (numStack.Count = 2 And opStack.Count >= 1) Then
         EvalExpression()
       End If
```

```
      ElseIf (obj = "+" Or obj = "-" Or obj = "*" _
            Or obj = "/" Or obj = "=") Then
        opStack.Push(obj)
      End If
    End Sub
    Private Sub EvalExpression()
      Dim op1, op2 As Double
      Dim operator As String
      op2 = CDbl(numStack.Pop())
      op1 = CDbl(numStack.Pop())
      operator = CStr(opStack.Pop())
      Select Case operator
        Case "+"
          result = op1 + op2
        Case "-"
          result = op1 - op2
        Case "*"
          result = op1 * op2
        Case "/"
          result = op1 / op2
      End Select
      numStack.Push(result)
    End Sub
    Public Function Show() As Double
      Return result
    End Function
    Public Sub Clear()
      result = 0
      numStack.Clear()
      opStack.Clear()
    End Sub
End Class
```

SUMMARY

Writing our calculator program using object-oriented techniques makes our program much easier to read, debug, and modify. The Calculator class that provides the substrate to our program is designed so that it can be used either as a Console application or as a Windows application. If we had not built a

Calculator class, we would have had to place the calculator code inside the Form1 class, making the program less efficient in every way.

EXERCISES

1. Add a +/− button to the calculator that is used to change the sign of the number in the display.
2. Implement a memory system that allows you to store a number in memory and then recall it later in a series of calculations.
3. Add a Sqrt button to the calculator that returns the square root of the number in the display.
4. Add a 1/× button to the calculator. When this button is pushed, the number displayed is a fraction representing the result of dividing 1 by the original number. For example, if the number in the display is 4, pressing 1/× returns 0.25.
5. Add a backspace button that removes the last entry in the display (which could be a digit or a decimal point).

CHAPTER 13

Database Programming Using ADO.NET

This chapter explains how to perform database programming in an object-oriented way. There are several techniques (patterns) we can use to make a VB.NET/ADO.NET program object-oriented. Many of these techniques were first discussed (though not necessarily first used) in Martin Fowler's book *Patterns of Enterprise Application Architecture* (Fowler 2003). This chapter will distill some of the patterns he presents into working code that a VB.NET programmer will recognize, especially a programmer who now understands OOP. First, though, we'll provide you with an overview of how to use ADO.NET to access data stored in a database.

AN OVERVIEW OF ADO.NET

ActiveX Data Objects.NET (ADO.NET) is an object-oriented database API that allows a programmer to use one set of classes to access many different types of databases.

ADO.NET Objects

ADO.NET consists of a set of classes that encapsulate the behavior of the different aspects of a database. These classes include objects that represent the database, individual tables, columns within tables, and rows in tables. There are also specialized objects for making database connections and database commands.

The following list highlights these objects

- DataSet represents a subset of a database and is a parent object to many of the other objects used in ADO.NET.
- DataTable is used to work with the contents of a single table.
- DataColumn is used to represent each column in a table.
- DataRow represents a row of data from a table. Row data are retrieved from the Rows collection of a DataTable object.
- DataAdapter is used as a bridge between a DataTable object and the physical data source, or database, the program is using.
- DBConnection represents a connection to a database.
- DBCommand represents SQL statements sent to the database through the connection.
- DBAdapter is used to moderate the work between the DataSet object and the database. Having a DBAdapter object allows a DataSet object to represent more than one data source, which can help keep resources low when working with multiple data sources.

ACCESSING A DATABASE TABLE USING NON-OOP TECHNIQUES

In this section we'll discuss the basics of connecting to and accessing data using ADO.NET. For this example, we'll be connecting to a local version of Microsoft's SQL Server, using the Northwind sample database. This example uses a very traditional, non-OOP style of coding. After this section, the balance of the chapter is dedicated to showing you how to use OOP techniques to perform the same database operations we perform in this section.

The classes we'll use for programming in ADO.NET are found in the System.Data and the System.Data.SQLClient namespaces, so you must import these namespaces into your program.

Making and Opening a Database Connection

The first step in accessing data in a database using ADO.NET is to create a connection object and a connection string. The connection object represents the physical connection between a VB.NET program and a database, and the connection string stores the commands necessary to open the database.

Once we have a connection object and connection string, we can open the connection between the database and the program by calling the connection object's Open method. The following code performs these tasks:

```
Dim connectionString As String = _
  "Data Source=localhost; Initial Catalog=Northwind;" _
  & "Integrated Security=True"
Dim connObject As SqlConnection = New _
  SqlConnection(connectionString) connObject.Open()
```

Filling the DataSet

The next step in accessing a database using ADO.NET is to fill a DataSet object with data from a table or tables. For this, we need a string variable that holds a SQL statement along with a DataAdapter object that serves as the intermediary between our program and the database.

Once these objects are set up, the next step is to use the DataAdapter object to fill the DataSet object with the data from the table. Here's the code:

```
Dim strSelect As String = "Select * From Customers"
Dim dAdapter As SqlDataAdapter = New _
  SqlDataAdapter(strSelect, connObject)
Dim dSet As DataSet = New DataSet()
dAdapter.Fill(dSet, "Customers")
```

Displaying Data

Data returned from a database table are stored in a DataTable object by rows. To be able to use the data in a program, you must access each row using a DataRow object. The DataTable object has a Rows collection that stores all the rows of the returned data. The DataRow object is used, in this example, to store each row from the Rows collection as it is retrieved using a For Each loop:

```
Dim dTable As DataTable = dSet.Tables("Customers")
Dim dRow As DataRow
For Each dRow In dTable.Rows
  Console.WriteLine(dRow("CompanyName") & _
    Constants.vbTab & dRow("ContactName"))
Next
```

Fields within a row are displayed by passing the field name to a DataRow object, as shown here. Alternatively, you can use the column index number of a field to display its data, like this:

```
For Each dRow In dTable.Rows
  Console.WriteLine(dRow(1) & Constants.vbTab & dRow(2))
Next
```

There are other ways to display data from a database table. ADO.NET also provides row-by-row control for moving through a data set. You can move freely through the Rows collection by specifying which row of the DataTable object you want to go through. The following code fragment demonstrates how this works:

```
Dim index As Integer
For index = 0 To dTable.Rows.Count - 1
  Console.WriteLine(dTable.Rows(index).Item(0) & " " & _
                    dTable.Rows(index).Item(1))
Next
```

Updating a Record

Updating a row in a data set is very straightforward. The DataRow class has methods for beginning and ending an editing session [BeginEdit() and EndEdit()]. In between these two methods, you make direct assignments to rows to change whatever data need to be changed.

The following code fragment demonstrates how this works:

```
Dim editRow As DataRow = dTable.Rows(0)
editRow.BeginEdit()
editRow("CompanyName") = "MyCo"
editRow.EndEdit()
```

Placing the code between the BeginEdit() and EndEdit() methods marks the row referenced in the code as currently being edited, which means that other processes can't access that particular row until the editing is complete.

The next step is to transfer the changed row from the data set, which is current only in memory, to the physical location of the table. Since the DataAdapter object is our link between the program and the database, we use that object to update the database by calling the Update method and passing in the DataSet object and the name of the table:

```
dAdapter.Update(dSet, "Customers")
```

To finalize the updating process, we need to tell the data set to accept the changes by calling the AcceptChanges method:

```
dSet.AcceptChanges()
```

Deleting a Record

The steps for deleting a record from a table are similar to those for updating a record. First, you must find the record you want to delete. Then you call the Delete method on the Row object to delete. Finally, you must update the database through the DataAdapter object and call the AcceptChanges method of the DataSet object.

Here is some code that deletes a given record:

```
Dim delRow As DataRow = dTable.Rows(4)
delRow.Delete()
dAdapter.Update(dSet, "Customers")
dSet.AcceptChanges()
```

Adding New Records

To add a new record to a table, you have to first create a new Row object. Once the object is created, you simply add data to each field in the row and then call the Add method of the DataTable object's Rows collection.

Let's add a new record to the Customers table to see how the code looks:

```
Dim addRow As DataRow = dTable.NewRow()
addRow("CustomerID") = "MICHM"
addRow("CompanyName") = "Michael's Exports"
addRow("ContactName") = "Michael McMillan"
addRow("ContactTitle") = "CEO"
addRow("Address") = "3000 W. Scenic"
addRow("City") = "North Little Rock"
addRow("PostalCode") = "72118"
addRow("Phone") = "501-812-0000"
dTable.Rows.Add(addRow)
dAdapter.Update(dSet, "Customers")
dSet.AcceptChanges()
```

This completes our review of the basics of ADO.NET. The next section discusses how to write ADO.NET code in an object-oriented way using the techniques developed by Martin Fowler and his colleagues.

OOP TECHNIQUES FOR DATABASE ACCESS

As we mentioned at the beginning of this chapter, the leading-edge work on database programming using OOP techniques is being done by Martin Fowler, as evidenced by his book *Patterns of Enterprise Application Architecture* (Fowler 2003).

In his book, Fowler describes a series of patterns useful in business programming, which primarily means that the patterns are used to connect an application program with a database or databases. The book describes over fifty patterns for database access and also for using the Web as a layer in the design architecture. In this chapter, we're going to limit our discussion to three or four of the patterns that are directly related to programming with ADO.NET.

The Table Data Gateway

The Table Data Gateway pattern provides the programmer with the means to encapsulate both the methods for accessing data in a database with data returned from the methods. Using the word "Table" is a little misleading here, since what we are really doing is returning a data set that is the basis for a DataTable object, as you learned earlier.

The Table Data Gateway is usually just a collection of methods that are used to retrieve data from a table, as well as update, insert, and delete records. No actual data are stored in a Table Data Gateway object. Retrieval methods return DataTable objects, which can be used in client code to examine the results. Insert, delete, and update methods are written as subroutines since they don't have return values.

A Table Data Gateway class first has to define a few Private data members. These members are used to make the connection to the database table. Using the Customers table from the Northwind database again, here is how we define the Private data members for a CustomersGateway class:

```
Imports System.Data
Imports System.Data.SqlClient

Public Class CustomersGateway

  Private connectionString As String = "Data _
    Source=localhost; Initial Catalog=Northwind;" _
    & "Integrated Security = True"

  Private connObject As SqlConnection = _
    New SqlConnection(connectionString)
```

The Imports statements are included to remind you that you need these namespaces imported into your program.

Next, we need a constructor method. All it has to do is open the connection, so it's a one-liner:

```
Public Sub New()
  connObject.Open()
End Sub
```

Now we can write some methods for returning data to our Table Data Gateway object. Let's start with the simplest SQL statement that returns all the data from the table. We'll call the method ReturnAll():

```
Public Function ReturnAll() As DataTable
   Dim strSelect As String = "Select * From Customers"
   Dim dAdapter As SqlDataAdapter = New _
    SqlDataAdapter(strSelect, connObject)
   Dim dSet As DataSet = New DataSet()
   dAdapter.Fill(dSet, "Customers")
   Dim dTable As DataTable = dSet.Tables("Customers")
   Return dTable
End Function
```

Let's look at some client code to see exactly how to use this class:

```
Sub main()
   Dim customers As New CustomersGateway()
   Dim custTable As DataTable = customers.ReturnAll()
   Dim dRow As DataRow
   Dim index As Integer
   For index = 0 To custTable.Rows.Count - 1
   ' Show just the first two columns
   Console.WriteLine(custTable.Rows(index).Item(0) _
    & " " & custTable.Rows(index).Item(1))
   Next
   Console.Read()
End Sub
```

This code is much cleaner than the example earlier in the chapter that uses standard programming techniques. Putting all the connecting code, etc. into the class lets the client concentrate on the job to be done. This is important because, as Fowler points out in his book, application programmers don't necessarily know how to write well-formed SQL statements. Having the SQL statements wrapped up in the Table Data Gateway class makes it easier for them to work on the application at hand.

The next method we'll develop is used to find a specific contact name from the Customers table. We call this method ReturnWithContactName and it accepts one argument—a name in String format. Here's the definition:

```
Public Function ReturnWithContactName(ByVal name As _
                                      String)
  Dim strSelect As String = "Select * From Customers _
   Where ContactName = " & "'" & name & "'"
  Dim dAdapter As SqlDataAdapter = New _
   SqlDataAdapter(strSelect, connObject)
  Dim dSet As DataSet = New DataSet()
  dAdapter.Fill(dSet, "Customers")
  Dim dTable As DataTable = dSet.Tables("Customers")
  Return dTable
End Function
```

A Table Data Gateway class needs a general method for finding column-specific data that isn't tied to any one particular column. This is handled using a Where clause in a SQL statement. We'll call this method ReturnWhere and here's the code:

```
Public Function ReturnWhere(ByVal clause As String)
  Dim strSelect As String = "Select * From Customers _
                             Where " & clause
  Dim dAdapter As SqlDataAdapter = _
   New SqlDataAdapter(strSelect, connObject)
  Dim dSet As DataSet = New DataSet()
  dAdapter.Fill(dSet, "Customers")
  Dim dTable As DataTable = dSet.Tables("Customers")
  Return dTable
End Function
```

A method to add a new row to a table must receive all its data in the method argument, like this:

```
Public Sub AddRow(ByVal id As String, ByVal compName _
 As String, ByVal contactName As String, ByVal title _
 As String, ByVal address As String, ByVal city As _
 String, ByVal zip As String, ByVal phone As String, _
 ByVal fax As String)

  Dim strSelect As String = "Select * From Customers"
  Dim dAdapter As SqlDataAdapter = New _
```

```
   SqlDataAdapter(strSelect, connObject)
  Dim dSet As DataSet = New DataSet()
  dAdapter.Fill(dSet, "Customers")
  Dim dTable As DataTable = dSet.Tables("Customers")
  Dim addRow As DataRow = dTable.NewRow()
  addRow("CustomerID") = id
  addRow("CompanyName") = compName
  addRow("ContactName") = contactName
  addRow("ContactTitle") = title
  addRow("Address") = address
  addRow("City") = city
  addRow("PostalCode") = zip
  addRow("Phone") = phone
  addRow("Fax") = fax
  dTable.Rows.Add(addRow)
  dAdapter.Update(dSet, "Customers")
  dSet.AcceptChanges()
End Sub
```

There are, of course, many other methods you can include in this class, but by now you should get the gist of it.

Frequently, a Table Data Gateway object is used in conjunction with a Table Module object. This object is used to perform the business logic on a set of data (one or more rows) returned by a Table Data Gateway object. We discuss the Table Module next.

The Table Module

The Table Module allows you to package data (from a database) with the application code that uses these data. This, of course, is the prime directive of OOP and is as much of a help when writing a database application as it is when writing any other type of application.

The Table Data Gateway pattern is used to package SQL statements that retrieve data sets together into one unit, whereas the Table Module pattern is used to perform data processing on one particular data set. We use a Table Data Gateway object to get the table we load into a Table Module object.

It is common to create a Table Module base class and to put all the table-specific functionality in a derived class. A Table Module base class, then, looks like this:

```
Public Class TableModule

  Protected table As DataTable

  Public Sub New(ByVal dTable As DataTable)
    table = dTable
  End Sub

End Class
```

Clearly, the base class doesn't do much; nor does it really have to, since, as we said, we want to put all the functionality for each Table Module class in derived classes.

Let's look at an example using a different table from the Northwind database—the Orders Detail table. The data contained in the table include an order id, the order placed, the unit price of the product, the quantity ordered, and the discount on the order, if any. Figure 13.1 shows a screenshot of the table.

To get a feel for how to use a Table Module object, let's write a program that calculates the total of all the orders in the Orders Detail table. We will create a derived class named OrderDetailModule that inherits from the TableModule class. The OrderDetailModule class gets its data table from an OrderDetailGateway class that passes a DataTable object to the OrderDetailModule. Here's the complete program:

```
Imports System.Data
Imports System.Data.SqlClient
Public Class OrderDetailGateway

  Private connectionString As String = _
   "Data Source=localhost; Initial Catalog = _
   Northwind;" & "Integrated Security = True"

  Private connObject As SqlConnection = New _
   SqlConnection(connectionString)

  Public Sub New()
```

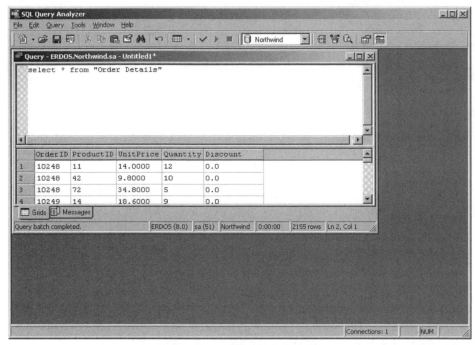

FIGURE 13.1. Orders Detail Table

```
    connObject.Open()
  End Sub

  Public Function ReturnAll() As DataTable
    Dim strSelect As String = "Select * From " & _
     """Order Details"""

    Dim dAdapter As SqlDataAdapter = New _
     SqlDataAdapter(strSelect, connObject)
    Dim dSet As DataSet = New DataSet()
    dAdapter.Fill(dSet, "OrderDetails")
    Dim dTable As DataTable = _
     dSet.Tables("OrderDetails")
    Return dTable
  End Function

End Class

Public Class TableModule
```

```
    Protected table As DataTable

    Public Sub New(ByVal dTable As DataTable)
      table = dTable
    End Sub

End Class

Public Class OrderDetailModule : Inherits TableModule

    Public Sub New(ByVal dTable As DataTable)
      MyBase.New(dTable)
    End Sub

    Public Function CalcTotal() As Double
      Dim total As Double
      Dim index As Integer
      For index = 0 To table.Rows.Count - 1
        total += table.Rows(index).Item("UnitPrice") * _
                 table.Rows(index).Item("Quantity")
      Next
      Return total
    End Function

End Class

Module module1

    Sub main()
      Dim ordDetail As New OrderDetailGateway()
      Dim orderDetail As New _
       OrderDetailModule(ordDetail.ReturnAll)
      Console.WriteLine("Total of all orders: " & _
       FormatNumber(orderDetail.CalcTotal(), 2))
      Console.Read()

    End Sub

End Module
```

Notice how little code is used in the code module. Earlier, without the Table Module class, we performed a similar task (looping through a DataTable) but needed several more lines of code. Using a Table Module object to encapsulate application code makes our resulting client code easier to write, easier to read, and, perhaps most importantly, easier to maintain.

SUMMARY

Database patterns such as the two covered here are becoming important tools for application programmers. Currently, Java programmers are benefiting the most from these tools because most of the books and articles discussing these tools are written in Java. Visual Basic.NET programmers can also benefit from these tools.

This chapter covered only two of the many enterprise application architecture patterns—i.e., patterns used in designing database-oriented software that are discussed in Fowler (2003). In the chapter on ASP.NET programming, we look at a few more of these patterns. Many more details are covered in Fowler's book and you should examine them if you are interested in database programming using VB.NET.

EXERCISES

1. Write a Windows application that uses a Table Data Gateway object and a Table Module object to display the fields from the Customers table of the Northwind database on a form.
2. Write a Windows application that uses a Table Data Gateway object and a Table Module object to access the Order Detail table of the Northwind database. The application should allow the user to display the order total for any one product id.

References

(Bloch 2001) Bloch, Joshua. *Effective Java Programming Language Guide*. Addison-Wesley, Boston, 2001.

(Budd 2002) Budd, Timothy A. *An Introduction to Object-Oriented Programming*, Third Edition, Addison-Wesley, Boston, 2002.

(Fowler 2000) Fowler, Martin. *Refactoring—Improving the Design of Existing Code*, Addison-Wesley, Boston, 2000.

(Fowler 2003) Fowler, Martin. *Patterns of Enterprise Application Architecture*, Addison-Wesley, Boston, 2003.

(Gamma 1995) Gamma, Erich, Richard Helm, Ralph Johnson, and John Vlissides. *Design Patterns—Elements of Reusable Object-Oriented Software*, Addison-Wesley, Reading, MA, 1995.

(Kay 1993) Kay, Alan C., "The Early History of Smalltalk," The Second ACM SIGPLAN History of Programming Languages Conference, *ACM SIGPLAN Notices* 28(3):69–75, March 1993.

Index